PRAISE FOR POTENTIAL-IZE

"As someone who has built a tech unicorn while relocating 1,000 employees during wartime, I can tell you that external success without internal development is a house built on sand. This book shows you how to develop the 'inner drive' to lead with clarity and courage in the AI age. The inner work changes everything."
—**Arsen Tomsky, Founder & CEO, in Drive**

"AI can lift us from scarcity to abundance, but POTENTIAL-IZE reminds us that technology should ride on humanity's coattails—not the other way around."
—**Joe Ward, Founder & CEO, Edge Video AI**

"A powerful and practical roadmap for thriving in an AI-driven world. Andrew Bryant shows us how to unlock the uniquely human potential that no algorithm can replicate."
—**Dorie Clark, executive education faculty at Columbia Business School and Wall Street Journal bestselling author of *The Long Game***

"The question too many are failing to ask in this frenetic race toward AI adoption, is "what are we also discovering about our own untapped potential to learn, grow and impact the present, along with shaping an unfamiliar future?" In this enlightening and actionable book, Andrew Bryant shows readers how to leverage and embrace a growing slate of available tools to significantly grow our leadership potential and shape our corner of the world, rather than passively abdicating that role to AI or others. Not for the faint of heart, Bryant lays out the hard work necessary to reach our unrecognized potential, individually, organizationally, and culturally. This is an important book. Highly recommended."
—**David Avrin, CSP, GSF, Author of *Ridiculously Easy to Do Business With* and *Why Customers Leave***

"I've long admired Andrew Bryant's thought leadership. At a time when artificial intelligence is redefining the workplace and even the meaning of human value, his unique perspective is indispensable.

Too often, leaders frame AI as a contest between humans and machines. That industrial-age mindset pushes organizations into a relentless pursuit of efficiency. They focus on creating operational competence at the expense of human distinction. The result? Short-term success, long-term vulnerability.

Bryant's new book, POTENTIAL-IZE, is a powerful corrective. This is not another survival guide for the AI era; it is a roadmap to transcendent success. Andrew Bryant demonstrates how AI can become a catalyst to amplify what makes us uniquely human: creativity, empathy, and the ability to inspire."
    —Scott McKain CEO, The Distinction Group;
        Author of ICONIC and Beyond Distinction

"Andrew Bryant's work on self-leadership has been cited in over 150 research papers. In POTENTIAL-IZE, he brilliantly expands this foundation to show how we can all achieve far more than we believe possible."
    —Dr. Tanvi Gautam

"POTENTIAL-IZE is a masterclass in what I call Human-to-Human leadership, where technology amplifies, but never replaces, our most human potential. Run, don't walk, to read this; it's the book that will sit beside you in every decision for years to come."
    —Bryan Kramer, Best-selling author of H2H:
        Human-to-Human, USA Today Bestseller, TED
            speaker, and 3-time CEO

"Every leader faces this reality: AI is reshaping what human work means, and yesterday's people development strategies won't cut it. Andrew Bryant's POTENTIAL-IZE gives leaders the specific tools to develop human potential alongside artificial intelligence... not despite it. If you're responsible for developing people in today's workplace, this comprehensive guide belongs on your desk."
    —Angus Nelson, Performance Architect | Founder & CEO,
        Evolve Leadership | Author & Keynote Speaker, Neuro
            Resilient Leader

POTENTIAL-IZE

POTENTIAL-IZE

How Leaders Unlock
Human Potential in the Age of AI

ANDREW BRYANT

*'The roadmap to thrive with AI, by unlocking what
makes us truly human.'*
Scott McKain, CEO of The Distinction Group

Registered office

John Wiley & Sons, Inc., 111 River Street, Hoboken, NJ 07030, USA
John Wiley & Sons Ltd, New Era House, 8 Oldlands Way, Bognor Regis, West Sussex, PO22 9NQ, UK

For details of our global editorial offices, customer services, and more information about Wiley products visit us at www.wiley.com.

The manufacturer's authorized representative according to the EU General Product Safety Regulation is Wiley-VCH GmbH, Boschstr. 12, 69469 Weinheim, Germany, e-mail: Product_Safety@wiley.com.

Library of Congress Cataloging-in-Publication Data:

ISBN 9781907312922 (paperback)
ISBN 9781907312939 (ePub)
ISBN 9781907312946 (ePDF)

Cover Design: Wiley
Cover Image: © Eric Schaeffer/Getty Images
Author Photo: Courtesy of Andrew Bryant

Printed and bound by CPI Group (UK) Ltd, Croydon, CR0 4YY

C9781907312922_171225

WHO IS THIS BOOK FOR?

If you've ever wondered whether you'll become irrelevant as AI grows more powerful, this book will show you that the opposite is true. You're standing at the most exciting moment in human history, when AI doesn't diminish human potential but amplifies it in ways we're only beginning to understand.

You need this book if you're:

A Leader Wrestling with AI Transformation. You are implementing AI in your organization, but sensing that pure efficiency isn't enough. You've heard the horror stories of companies that automated their way to customer dissatisfaction and employee disengagement. You want to harness AI's power while amplifying, not diminishing, human capabilities. You need frameworks for creating environments where both artificial and human intelligence flourish.

A Professional Feeling the Ground Shift. Your industry is changing faster than your ability to keep up. You see AI handling tasks that used to require human expertise, and you're wondering what your unique value proposition will be. You need practical strategies for developing skills that become more valuable alongside AI rather than being replaceable by it.

A Manager Responsible for Developing Others. You are tasked with unlocking potential in your team, but traditional performance management feels inadequate for this moment. You need new approaches that help people discover capabilities they didn't know they possessed and develop resilience for an uncertain future.

An Executive Coach or HR Professional. Your clients are navigating career transitions in an AI-disrupted world. They need more than resume polishing or interview skills; they need fundamental reframing of how to approach professional development when the rules keep changing.

An Entrepreneur Building for Tomorrow. You are creating something new and need people who can think, adapt, and grow with your vision. You understand that hiring for yesterday's skills won't build tomorrow's company. You need frameworks for identifying and developing the human potential that drives innovation.

An Individual Committed to Growth. You have read enough self-help books to know that quick fixes don't create lasting change. You want systematic approaches to developing your potential that go beyond motivation and positive thinking to create genuine capability and resilience.

WHAT YOU WILL GAIN

By the end of this book, you'll have:

- **A clear framework (IGNITE)** for systematic human development in the AI age.
- **Practical tools** for identifying and developing potential in yourself and others.

- **Real-world examples** of individuals and organizations thriving through human–AI collaboration.
- **Assessment methods** for tracking growth across multiple dimensions of human capability.
- **Strategic approaches** for hiring, developing, and leading in an AI-transformed world.

A WARNING AND A PROMISE

The Warning: This book requires effort. The concepts are straightforward, but application demands consistent practice. If you're looking for passive consumption or quick fixes, this isn't for you.

The Promise: If you commit to implementing these frameworks, you'll develop capabilities that make you more valuable as AI becomes more powerful. You'll become someone who doesn't just adapt to change but helps others transform through it.

This book is for people who understand that the future belongs not to those who compete with AI but to those who can amplify human potential through strategic partnerships with AI.

Your potential is calling. The question is: are you ready to answer?

ABOUT THE AUTHOR

Andrew Bryant is a global authority on self-leadership and the founder of Self Leadership International. His research on autonomy, responsibility, and intentionally influencing thinking, feelings, and actions has been cited in over 150 academic papers and PhD dissertations across multiple disciplines.

English by birth, Australian by passport, Brazilian by wife, lived in Asia, Andrew now resides in Portugal, but has worked with clients and spoken to audiences in over 40 countries.

Andrew is a Global Citizen with a passion for awakening people to their potential, regardless of the circumstances of their birth.

This is Andrew's fifth book; his previous works have focused on communication, self-leadership, and leadership.

In addition to writing and giving speeches, Andrew " makes leaders better" as an executive coach to senior executives and facilitates the development of executive leadership teams.

Andrew believes and teaches that leadership is a conversation, a one-to-one or one-to-many conversation that leads to the right behaviors.

Andrew graduated as a physiotherapist in 1982 and as an acupuncturist in 1985. After two years working for a London teaching hospital, he gravitated to private practice and working with athletes and sportspeople.

Physiotherapy taught Andrew curiosity and observation, and he learned the maxim:

Prescription without diagnosis is malpractice

This maxim and his skills served him well as he pivoted from working with athletes to working with disruptive Silicon Valley startups and complex multinationals.

In addition to physiotherapy and acupuncture, Andrew studied hypnosis, neurosemantics, coaching, psychology, and leadership. His underlying curiosity has always been about what makes a difference to human potential. This focus led him to do research, resulting in his 2012 book *Self Leadership: How to Become a More Successful, Efficient, and Effective Leader from the Inside Out* (Bryant & Kazan, 2012) with Dr. Ana Kazan.

In 2007, he achieved the prestigious Certified Professional Speaker designation. He is a past President of Asia Professional Speakers Singapore (2015–2016) and The Professional Speakers Association of Spain (2021–2023).

Andrew is proud of his work coaching self-leadership for disadvantaged teenagers and executive presence to women leaders.

Andrew volunteers as a mentor for the Women's Leader Circle, empowering the next generation of women leaders.

His values are respect, ownership, and impact (ROI); he loves traveling, hiking, and playing chess.

If you have a conference, convention, or leadership offsite and would like to engage Andrew, he can be reached through selfleadership.com or linkedin.com/in/andrewbryant.

DEDICATION

This book is dedicated to my wife, Andrea, who has always seen my potential, even when I doubted it myself.

I want to thank my friend and fellow speaker, Fredrik Haren, who helped me realize that potentialize has been my "inner theme" throughout my career and encouraged me to write this book.

Organizational psychologist Dr. Paul Englert has also earned my gratitude for his constant challenges to my thinking and for supporting me in developing my self-leadership theories and methodologies.

Thank you to colleagues and thought leaders who allowed me to pick their brains: Aaron Phipps, Adhisha Dahanayake, Andy Lopata, Anneliese Olson, Anupama Lal, Artem Ivanenko, Brooks Cole, Caryn Davies, Chidinma Raymond-Limejuice, Christopher M. Barlow (PhD), Dalia Turner, Diane Hamilton, Dorie Clark, Erik Vermeulen, Gareth Lock, Herdis Pala Palsdottir, Jessica Fontana, Kevin Gaskell, Magor Csibi, Manish Bundhun, Marica Reynolds, Marina Traub, Mark Colbourne, Melissa Goldner, Olivier Malafronte, Radu Palamariu, Reverend "Stevo" Stephenson, Rohit Talwar, Ruth Gotian, Scott McArthur, Shane Kidwell, Sherif Elogeiry, Sophia Aguilar, Steve Cadigan, Steve Judge, Tanvi Gautam, and Wanda Naomi Rau.

To my children, Tasha, Nathan, and Laila – I see your potential and dedicate this book to you. May you achieve everything that you can imagine.

FOREWORD

You can measure a company by what it optimizes for. Too often, we chase speed and cost and then wonder why trust, creativity, and loyalty feel thin. People are not a cost line; they are the engine. This book argues for something simple and brave: design your business so people can potentialize, and let technology amplify that—not erase it.

There are many reasons this book matters right now. The noise about AI has pushed leaders into a false choice. Automate, or stay human. Andrew Bryant refuses that trap. He gives us language and a method to do both well. Potentialize means perform at your best while expanding what your best can be. I find that deeply practical. It is not another pep talk; it is a user manual for leaders who actually own outcomes.

What I like most is how unapologetically human the approach is. The story of a bus driver in Sydney who chooses his attitude on a wet morning is not just a story; it is a standard. Leadership begins inside. If we do not lead our thoughts and responses, we will not lead anyone else. At People Matters, we see the same pattern in organizations that scale with soul. Self-leadership first, then team leadership, then systems.

This book also calls out a truth many of us have learned the hard way. "Follow your passion" sounds inspiring, but it often keeps people stuck. Competence creates passion.

Build skill, earn small wins, then passion arrives on its own. That is how you build talent markets that last.

On AI, my opinion is clear. Tools are not the strategy. Your advantage is how your people think, decide, and connect. Bryant's idea of "riding the dragon" is the right posture. Use AI to multiply judgment, creativity, and care. Do not outsource them. The moment you hand your human edge to a machine because it seems cheaper this quarter, you start losing ground that you cannot win back next year.

The frameworks here travel well from page to practice. IGNITE gives leaders a full stack to work with: inspire a real story, guide with mentorship and feedback, nurture belief and belonging, integrate human strengths with AI, transform adversity into growth, and evaluate relentlessly. If you run HR, these are not posters. They are your operating system. If you run a P&L, that's how you de-risk culture while you scale.

I also appreciate the honesty about efficiency versus effectiveness. Many teams have learned that a faster response is not the same as better relationships. Customers remember presence. Colleagues remember how they felt after a tough conversation. Performance equals potential minus interference. Your job as a leader is to remove that interference and set the conditions where people can do the best work of their lives, together.

You will find stories that stick. An athlete who rebuilds identity after a brutal accident. A founder who realizes his energy was survival, not purpose, and then rewires his work to serve something bigger than himself. These are not glossy case studies. They read like field notes from real change, with all the mess that growth requires.

If you lead hiring, Chapter 11 will likely make you nod. Hire for tomorrow, not yesterday. Stop playing Tetris with CVs. Look for learning velocity, drive, ethics, and the ability to collaborate with AI. Teach the rest. This is how you future-proof capability without burning people out. It is also how you build opportunity that is fair.

Let me say something that might sound unfashionable. Culture is not free snacks and all hands. Culture is the thousands of choices your managers make when no one is watching. This book gives those managers language, tools, and the courage to choose better. The exercises at the end of chapters are short, but if you do them, your Monday will change. So will your next one on one.

Read this with a pen. Mark the parts that make you uncomfortable. Try one idea per week with your team. Ask people what got easier, what got more meaningful. Keep what works, discard what doesn't. That is how transformation really happens, quietly, inside the work.

Potential is not a promise. It is a responsibility. Leaders do not just extract performance, they expand it. If you believe that people are your greatest asset, prove it. Potential-ize is a very good place to start.

With respect,
Pushkaraj Bidwai
CEO, People Matters

CONTENTS

LIST OF FIGURES

PART I

WHY UNLOCK POTENTIAL?

THE FOUNDATION

In Part I, we will explore why your potential matters more now than ever. You will discover the archaeology of what makes us human: our ability to dream, create meaning, and transform adversity into wisdom. This isn't about adding buzzwords to your LinkedIn profile. This is about recognizing that authentic human intelligence becomes infinitely precious in a world of artificial intelligence.

> "Ongoing learning is critical to staying relevant. You must continue to update your skills."
> — Mark Cuban

CHAPTER 1

WHY POTENTIAL-IZE MATTERS

"The future belongs to those who understand that technology amplifies human intention, not replaces human purpose"

– Sundar Pichai

What if the greatest threat to human potential isn't artificial intelligence (AI), but our own assumptions about what potential actually means?

Most people think of potential as a seed waiting for the right conditions to grow. This metaphor is dangerously passive. I prefer to think of potential like groundwater beneath a desert landscape. From the surface, you see only cracked earth and sparse vegetation, suggesting limitation and scarcity. But hidden below lies an untapped reservoir that can gush to the surface and transform the entire ecosystem.

Have you considered what is required to allow your untapped reservoir of potential to transform?

As you wake up to news that another overnight AI breakthrough has made headlines – a chatbot passing the bar exam, a robot performing another surgery, an algorithm composing symphonies – somewhere in your mind a voice whispers: "What's left for humans to do?"

Potential is not just about individual or group achievement. It is about fundamental sovereignty and agency, the ability to act with choice and humanity in a world where machines can increasingly act for us.

The word potential comes from the Latin *potens*, meaning power. Your potential is not just what might be possible for you, but also your capacity to shape what is possible for everyone around you.

Efficiency is Not Effectiveness

Performance leads to efficiency, but potential is effectiveness; this is why Klarna CEO's recent decision matters so much.

Sebastian Siemiatkowski probably thought he'd unlocked Klarna's efficiency. In February 2024, their AI assistant was handling 2.3 million customer service conversations, doing the work of 700 full-time human agents. The spreadsheets sang. The board smiled.

But by year's end, Klarna was quietly rehiring humans; not because the AI had failed, but because they had discovered something crucial about human potential – efficiency is not always effective. When a loved one passes, your spouse leaves you, or your business fails, you don't want processing, you want presence. You don't need optimization, you need understanding.

An AI system can efficiently process patient intake forms in 30 seconds versus 5 minutes for a human nurse. It can perfectly categorize symptoms, assign priority scores, and route patients to appropriate departments based on protocols, but is it always effective? Imagine your 82-year-old mother at 2 a.m., confused and scared, saying only, "something is wrong."

The AI efficiently categorizes her as "non-urgent" based on her vague symptoms and stable vitals, but you share with the nurse that this behavior is completely new and not her baseline behavior. The nurse's experience and intuition reveal early-stage sepsis that could have been fatal if treated as "non-urgent."

Klarna's reversal reveals a profound tension at the heart of our technological moment. We stand at the intersection of unprecedented efficiency and irreplaceable humanity, and most leaders believe they must choose one or the other.

THE BEAUTIFUL CONTRADICTION OF OUR TIME

Here is the question keeping executives awake at night: "How do you harness AI's extraordinary capabilities without eliminating the human elements that create loyalty, innovation, and sustained success?"

Most leaders believe they face a binary choice: resist AI to preserve human connection or embrace it and accept the trade-offs, but there is a third path, to potentialize, and that is what we shall explore in this book.

Visionary leaders recognize a counterintuitive truth: the more AI can do, the more valuable distinctly human capabilities become. Industry analysts consistently observe that companies combining AI automation with enhanced human development outperform those pursuing automation alone.

As algorithms handle routine tasks, uniquely human skills (emotional intelligence, creative problem-solving, the ability to inspire and connect) don't just remain important; they become the primary source of competitive advantage.

But unlocking and unleashing this potential requires a fundamentally different approach: not just managing people more efficiently, but igniting their capacity to grow, adapt, and create. This is a value that no algorithm can replicate.

WHY THIS MATTERS RIGHT NOW

Mistakes are being made. Automation and AI are shiny toys that promise an increase in speed with cost reductions, but as you will discover in the pages of this book, they can only replace human performance. The missed opportunity is for this revolution to be an amplifier of human potential, so that human + AI can ignite a bright future.

The leaders and organizations that will thrive will not be those who choose between human and AI. They will be those who understand how to develop both simultaneously, creating conditions where human potential flourishes precisely because AI handles what machines do best (processing, analyzing, optimizing) as humans focus on what they do best (connecting, inspiring, innovating). This will require leaders who can navigate a fundamental shift: from managing productivity to unleashing potential; from optimizing systems to developing people; from measuring efficiency to inspiring excellence.

The stakes could not be higher. Companies that get this wrong will be trapped in the efficiency paradox: operationally successful but strategically vulnerable. Those who get it right will unlock and unleash potential they didn't know existed, in themselves and everyone around them.

Organizations have approximately two years to master this balance before permanent competitive disadvantages become fixed. Those who wait might find themselves operationally efficient but strategically irrelevant.

This book is your guide to becoming the kind of leader who doesn't just survive the AI revolution but leverages it to potentialize human capabilities in ways previously unimaginable. In a world of infinite optimization, the most valuable skill isn't efficiency; it is the ability to uncover, unlock, and unleash the potential in yourself and the people you lead.

In the pages ahead, you'll discover how to develop the self-leadership skills that AI cannot replicate (Part I), practical frameworks for maximizing human potential alongside AI (Part II), and strategies for inspiring excellence in others during technological transformation (Part III).

POTENTIAL-IZE

Now you know why we need a new word for our new reality.

Potential-ize: the art of performing at your best while continuously expanding what "your best" means. Unlike "maximize" (which assumes you'll eventually hit a ceiling), potentializing recognizes that human capability is fundamentally open-ended.

- When we have an idea, we conceptualize it.
- When we decide something is important, we prioritize it.
- When we want to make the best of something, we maximize it.
- And when we bring the best of ourselves to a situation, we **potential-ize** it!

(But from here on, I am going to drop the hyphen and use "potentialize")

BEYOND QUICK FIXES

It has been said that we are drowning in information but starving for transformation. We have more tools for self-improvement and professional development than any generation in history, more opportunities for education and advancement, and more examples of human achievement to inspire us.

Yet rates of anxiety, depression, loneliness, and existential confusion have never been higher.

Why do we feel most lost when we have the most options?

Was the Buddha right when he said, "Where there is choice, there is pain"?

Perhaps we have become addicted to quick fixes for whatever ails us, when the truth is that finding and developing potential is a journey.

The ideas, models, and stories in this book are intended to guide you on this journey because I have discovered that **potential is not a problem to solve but a tension to navigate.**

You, me, and everyone else has potential, but you can't measure it, and although it is valuable, you can't cash it in at the bank. Potential only becomes a currency when it helps you navigate adversity and achieve a desired outcome.

NOT LIVING UP TO YOUR POTENTIAL

"You have so much potential," said my teacher. Even at a young age, I understood that this was code for, "You could do so much more if you tried."

You probably had a similar experience because almost everyone I speak to shares this sense of their own potential.

Dorie Clark told me, "I was probably eight or nine, and I remember going around with my cousin who had a paper route, and I was visiting him for part of the summer, and so I tagged along while he was delivering newspapers and we met one of his newspaper clients, and I introduced myself, and I said, 'I'm Dorie Clark.' And he said, 'Oh, Dorie Clark, that sounds like a movie star name.' And I remember thinking, that's right. Yes. I didn't exactly end up going to Hollywood, but I remembered thinking, yeah, there is something special about that, about me."

Dorie went to university at 14, graduated at 18, and is now a Colombia business professor and *Wall Street Journal* best-selling author, so she is something special.

Do you feel special? Do you inspire others to feel special?

"I have all these ideas, but I don't put them into action," confessed a colleague of mine.

I have lost count of the number of my coaching clients who have told me, "My biggest fear is not living up to my potential."

One could argue that this obsession with "unlocking potential" is just a post-Enlightenment Protestant work ethic. Perhaps the rise of the self-help industry is another form of religion. Concepts like "finding your purpose" and "becoming your best self" may descend directly from religious notions of calling and spiritual transformation. Characters like Tony Robbins and Oprah could be viewed as secular preachers, and the entire self-help industry represents a displaced religious impulse in our secular age.

Initially, I believed the feeling of unrealized potential was an expression of impostor syndrome. Impostor syndrome is self-doubt regarding intellect, skills, or accomplishments among high-achieving individuals. It arises from negatively comparing oneself to others. However, further investigation revealed that this feeling is an internal drive, hard to articulate but tangible; there is more that we are capable of.

Do you feel it? Do you feel that you could be more and do more?

Potential means having or showing the capacity to develop into something in the future

I acknowledge the cultural component of potential. Although I was born and raised in the West, I spent 18 years in Asia. Rather than viewing potential as something to be "unlocked" or "maximized," Buddhism sees it as our fundamental nature that must be "uncovered" or "revealed."

In the West, we tend to measure potential in terms of achievement, whereas the prevailing Eastern belief is that every being has the potential for enlightenment.

Whether potential means unlocking or uncovering, the business imperative remains the same: developing human capabilities that complement rather than compete with AI.

But what are we capable of? What are the biological, economic, and other limitations?

How do we unlock or uncover our potential and release the potential of others?

How will we unlock the potential of that human + AI collaboration?

Introducing IGNITE

After studying hundreds of leaders who have successfully made the transition, I discovered they all follow, often unconsciously, six interconnected principles that form what I call the IGNITE framework. See Figure 1.1.

Figure 1.1   The IGNITE Model for Potential

Some leaders stumble into one or two of these principles by accident. The transformational leaders master all
six. They don't just survive the AI revolution; they use it to
unlock potential they didn't know existed.

I will briefly introduce this framework here, but relax,
you don't have to memorize the six principles. We will
refer to them repeatedly within each chapter, and they will
become second nature to you later in the book.

IGNITE: Your Roadmap to Potentialize

Here is an overview of the elements as applied to your personal journey.

- INSPIRE: Find your spark and take control of your story.
- GUIDE: Navigate with wisdom through mentorship
  and feedback.
- NURTURE: Create conditions for growth through
  belief and belonging.

- INTEGRATE: Combine human intelligence with AI capabilities.
- TRANSFORM: Turn challenges into catalysts for development.
- EVALUATE: Sustain and scale your impact through continuous learning.

The framework isn't a checklist to complete; it is a dynamic system that adapts to your situation. Sometimes you'll start with INSPIRE, sometimes with TRANS-FORM. The power lies in understanding how all six elements work together to unlock potential in yourself and others.

We can also use IGNITE as a diagnostic tool to see where we have gone off course. For example, Klarna's "all-in on bots" strategy inspired efficiency but not human empa-thy. They may have lacked a guide to navigate the human + AI transition, and there was little or no psychological safety for employees facing job displacement. In hindsight, they failed to integrate; AI replaced rather than ampli-fied humans. They did transform the business but when they evaluated their metrics, they had traded efficiency for effectiveness.

I want to celebrate Sebastian Siemiatkowski's courage to admit they went off course; most CEOs would try to bury that news. Now we can be inspired by this story and evaluate our own journey.

TRY THIS

Your Human Edge Inventory

- What do you do that requires human judgment, creativity, or emotional intelligence?
- When do people specifically seek you out (not just your role)?
- What problems do you solve that aren't in any manual or database?

Your Potentializing Vision

Rate yourself (1–10) on each element of IGNITE.

- **Inspire:** Do you have a clear sense of purpose?
- **Guide:** Are you actively seeking mentors or guidance?
- **Nurture:** Do you feel you belong and believe in yourself?
- **Integrate:** How well do you leverage AI and other tools?
- **Transform:** Are you regularly challenging yourself?
- **Evaluate:** Do you reflect on and adjust your approach?

Reflection: Write one sentence to complete the following: "To potentialize in the age of AI, I most need to. . ."

IT'S TIME FOR A NEW STORY

From our earliest days, we've been given scripts – narratives from well-meaning parents, teachers, and bosses. We hear stories that shape our beliefs about who we are and how the world functions. But with the tsunami of change approaching – technological, cultural, and organizational – continuing to live someone else's story isn't just limiting; it's dangerous.

We must become the authors of our own stories to ride the wave rather than be drowned by it. Our stories make us authentically human. When we tell stories, we don't simply relate sequences of events; we weave meaning, emotion, and significance into experiences.

Our stories emerge from the texture of being embodied in the world, feeling pain, desire, love, loss, and wonder. Our narratives build upon generations of shared wisdom, values, and traditions that shape our understanding of ourselves. Through stories, we make sense of our existence, creating purpose in a universe that doesn't readily offer obvious meaning. Storytelling creates bonds between teller and listener; we recognize ourselves in others' experiences and develop empathy. Our personal narratives define who we are, integrating the past and present into a coherent self.

Artificial intelligence can undoubtedly generate compelling text that mimics stories, but it lacks the embodied experience, personal stakes, cultural inheritance, and existential need that drive human storytelling. AI cannot love; it has no childhood memories, experiences of triumph or despair, and fear of death or hope for transcendence, which fuels our most profound narratives.

Perhaps what makes us distinctively human is not just the ability to tell stories but the necessity of doing so, our fundamental need to transform experience into narrative as we search for meaning in our finite existence.

But as Ayrton Senna's story reminds us, even the most compelling personal narratives require wisdom to guide them.

A CAUTIONARY TALE

Potential without wisdom can be dangerous. On May 1, 1994, potential met a concrete barrier at 135 miles per hour on lap seven of the San Marino Grand Prix at the Imola circuit in Italy. Driving for the Williams-Renault team, Ayrton Senna da Silva collided with a concrete barrier while taking the high-speed Tamburello corner. The impact was devastating and fatal, as the front right wheel and suspension penetrated the cockpit area.

Senna is regarded as one of the greatest drivers of all time in F1 motor racing. Over 11 seasons, from 1984 to 1994, he won three Formula One Driver's Championship titles and 41 Grand Prix.

Senna seemed wired to drive fast. In interviews, he spoke about how time was too slow for him, and this perception gave him the capacity to react faster than other drivers. Many young boys might dream of being racing car drivers, but Senna had the opportunity to realize his potential. Born into a wealthy Brazilian family, he learned to drive a jeep around his family's farm at age seven. Ayrton Senna had the willingness, capacity, and opportunity to unlock potential, maximize performance, and inspire excellence. In Senna's case, this came at the ultimate cost, and we can pause to ask: "Do we have potential, or does our potential have us?"

ARE YOU READY TO START YOUR JOURNEY?

You are standing at an inflection point that won't wait. Every day you delay potentializing, competitors who understand this balance pull further ahead. Every week your organization operates without this integration, you lose ground that becomes harder to recover.

The question isn't whether AI will reshape your industry, it already has. The question is whether you'll be among the leaders who harness this transformation to unlock unprecedented human potential, or among those who get left behind optimizing for a game that no longer exists.

Your potential has been waiting. The tools to develop it are in your hands. The only question remaining is: What story will you choose to write?

CHAPTER 2

FROM PASSENGER TO DRIVER: THE SHIFT TO POTENTIALIZE

"Mastering others is strength; mastering oneself is true power"

– Lao Tsu

On a cloudy Tuesday morning in Sydney, I learned the difference between circumstances and choice, and that leadership starts with leading yourself.

It's the year 2000, and I'm standing at a bus stop after losing everything that I thought mattered. Twelve months earlier, I had been wealthy, successful, and clear about my goals. Now, I had lost my business, was broke, and lost in a fog of despair. The rain started falling. I didn't have an umbrella, and my mood didn't improve.

The bus arrived, the doors wheezed open, and I was hit with an almost offensively cheerful: "Isn't it a great day!"

I had my misery speech rehearsed, chapter and verse, on why this was categorically not a great day. I'd lost my business, my bank account looked like a crime scene, and now

I was getting rained on without an umbrella. But something in that driver's authentic enthusiasm stopped me cold.

Here was a man with zero control over his route, schedule, or the weather. Yet he owned his response to all of it. Without any formal authority, his attitude transformed every person who stepped onto that bus, including me.

This encounter jogged me out of my fog. I understood a fundamental truth: we always have a choice. We can be the drivers of our lives or passengers, letting circumstances control our experience.

Following that encounter, I reframed my business failure as education and reconnected with my potential. I set out on the journey that became my life's work: understanding how people can unlock potential, lead themselves, and influence others.

That moment on the bus sparked a question that would consume the next decade of my life: if one person's choice to lead themselves could transform an entire busload of strangers, what would happen if we all learned this skill?

This encounter ignited my curiosity about human potential and led me to discover what I now call self-leadership.

WHY SELF-LEADERSHIP CHANGES EVERYTHING

Fast forward a few years, and my research and articles on self-leadership came to the attention of Dr. Ana Kazan on the other side of the world. Recognizing our shared passions, Ana and I agreed to collaborate on research and write a book on the topic (Bryant & Kazan, 2012).

Fun story: Ana is from Brazil, and although I am married to a Brazilian, Ana and I have never met in person; we collaborated virtually.

In the book, we defined self-leadership as "the practice of intentionally influencing your thinking, feelings, and actions toward your objectives."

Think of self-leadership as mental hygiene, something you practice daily, not a one-time intervention. Most people let their thoughts run wild, like unsupervised toddlers in a candy store. Self-leaders choose to be the adult in the "room" of their own minds.

Self-leadership is about taking ownership of your life and being authentically human. It is not a prescription for perfection but a wake-up call to take agency in choosing our attitude and actions.

What distinguishes a self-leader is this: regardless of circumstances, they exercise their autonomy by taking responsibility for themselves, while others blame, complain, and play the victim.

Self-leaders have stepped out of the fog and:

- Choose personal values and beliefs.
- Take responsibility for choices and outcomes.
- Step back and examine assumptions.
- Operate from an internal locus of control rather than external authority.

With self-leadership, we become the "driver" rather than "the passenger" as we exercise the power to choose our own thoughts and feelings and not be slaves to them.

By practicing self-leadership, we can transcend the stimulus–response lives of Pavlov's dogs or the conditioning of Skinner's pigeons. Instead, we can hold multiple perspectives simultaneously, embrace paradox and contradiction, evolve our identity, and influence change.

This does not mean self-leaders don't react or have the occasional meltdown; we are all human, but the self-leader can quickly get back in control.

Here's why this matters more than ever: we come into this world without any choice about the time and place of our birth, our parents, our DNA, or our early education. Our environment essentially "authors" us in the beginning. **But as we mature, we can exercise autonomy to become the authors of our lives.**

That last statement has a caveat, and we must pause to take a short philosophical and neuroscience detour to understand why.

THE ILLUSION OF "SELF"

For years after that bus ride, I believed transformation was about willpower and positive thinking. Then I discovered something that changed everything: the "self" I thought I was changing doesn't exist as I imagined.

Neuroscientists such as Sam Harris and Robert Sapolsky suggest our sense of being a conscious agent is essentially an illusion. But here's what my friend, organizational psychologist Dr. Paul Englert, helped me understand: if your identity is constructed rather than fixed, it's also editable.

Think about it this way: your past programming doesn't have to trap you. Your identity is a story you are actively writing, not a sentence you're serving. This insight transforms everything about potential:

- Your limitations are often just narratives, not natural laws.
- Your identity is more fluid than you think, but it filters everything you perceive.
- Agency comes from conscious authorship of your story.

As psychologist Daniel Gilbert notes: "The greatest achievement of the human brain is its ability to imagine objects and episodes that do not exist in the realm of the real, and it is this ability that allows us to think about the future."

Figure 2.1 illustrates how our sense of self is a fluid process. Our identity is influenced by our feelings, which come from our bodies. Our story is influenced by our memories, which are in turn influenced by our culture.

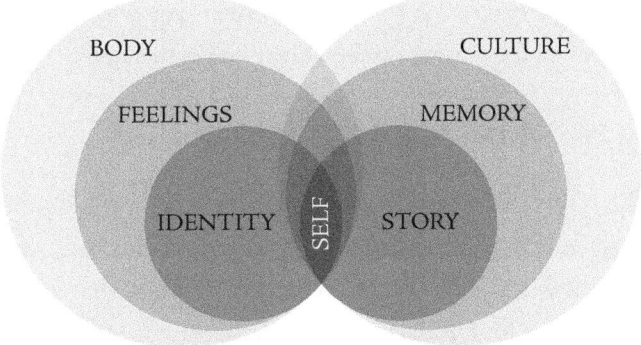

Figure 2.1 The Fluid Self

Figure 2.2 The Three Pillars of Self-Leadership

This insight shows we have multiple ways to upgrade our "self": by changing our stories, reindexing our identity, accessing our feelings, editing our memories, working our body, and choosing how we align with our culture.

If your sense of self is editable, how do you do that? After years of research and working with thousands of clients, I've discovered that self-leadership rests on three interconnected pillars. See Figure 2.2. If you master these, you will have the foundation for everything else we explore in this book.

THE THREE PILLARS OF SELF-LEADERSHIP

The IGNITE framework you learned in Chapter 1 is your roadmap for potentializing in the AI age. But, like any journey, you need a reliable vehicle to navigate that roadmap. The Three Pillars of Self-Leadership are that vehicle, your internal foundation that makes every element of IGNITE possible.

SELF-AWARENESS: KNOW THYSELF

"Know Thyself" was inscribed on an arch in the fore-court of the Temple of Apollo in Delphi, located on the southwestern slope of Mount Parnassus, around the 6th century BCE. This enduring maxim for self-examination and achieving potential has inspired thinkers throughout recorded history.

Self-awareness has two components:

1. **Internal self-awareness.** Understanding your own internal narratives, values, passions, aspirations, and reactions.
2. **External self-awareness.** Understanding how others see you and your impact on them.

Self-awareness is the starting point for effective leadership because self-aware leaders make better decisions, build stronger relationships, and create more positive workplace environments.

Practical techniques for developing greater self-awareness include mindfulness practices, seeking feedback, journaling, and psychometric assessment tools.

Self-awareness enables multiple IGNITE elements. You can't INSPIRE without knowing your values and natural strengths to help you craft a compelling vision, rather than chasing someone else's definition of success.

Self-awareness provides the baseline to meaningfully EVALUATE. You can only measure growth when you clearly understand your starting point and patterns.

Understanding yourself is just the beginning. Once you can see your patterns clearly, the next step is learning to choose your response rather than defaulting to reaction. This is where self-regulation comes in.

SELF-REGULATION: MASTER YOUR RESPONSES

Self-regulation is effectively managing your emotions, thoughts, and behaviors, especially in challenging situations. With self-regulation, we avoid impulsive reactions and can maintain focus on our goals. Self-regulation is not about suppressing emotions but choosing how to respond to them.

Self-regulation includes self-motivation and self-discipline. Practical techniques for improving self-regulation include owning our emotions, cognitive reframing, and physical techniques like controlled breathing.

To GUIDE requires self-regulation. Defensiveness, ego, and emotional reactivity block the ability to receive feedback and face uncomfortable truths.

Self-regulation allows us to TRANSFORM by turning challenges into catalysts and setbacks into development opportunities.

If we are to INTEGRATE and work effectively with AI, we must self-regulate to overcome anxiety and frustration with the change process.

As we regulate ourselves, we can learn.

SELF-LEARNING: EMBRACE CONTINUOUS GROWTH

In our rapidly changing world, the willingness and ability to learn continuously aren't just helpful, they are essential for survival. This means intentional learning, reflective practices, and maintaining what psychologist Carol Dweck calls a "growth mindset."

Continuous learning will NURTURE expanding potential, yours and others.

Self-learning ensures that each IGNITE element evolves rather than becomes static. Your ability to inspire grows, your integration with AI improves, and your transformation methods become more sophisticated.

The judicious use of AI can powerfully enhance self-regulation and self-learning by providing tools to analyze journaling, after-action reviews, and creating dedicated reflection time for deepening learning.

You might be wondering: "This all sounds good in theory, but how much can I change? Don't our genetics and upbringing limit us?" It's a fair question, and the answer might surprise you.

While you didn't choose your genes, you have far more influence over how they express themselves than most people realize.

YOUR DNA ISN'T YOUR DESTINY

"It is not in the stars to hold our destiny but in ourselves"
— William Shakespeare

True, we are "framed" from birth; we don't choose our DNA or our culture, but here is the fascinating truth — while you didn't choose your genes, you can influence how they behave. Think of your DNA as a vast library, and epigenetics as the librarian who decides which books get pulled from the shelves. Your choices – what you eat, how you handle stress, whether you exercise – tell that librarian which genetic "books" to open and which to keep closed.

In other words, you can turn genes "on" or "off" through behavioral choices, almost like choosing your favorite shows on Netflix or creating a Spotify playlist.

Your choices, each day, are rewriting your genetic code. When you exercise, you're not just building muscle but activating genes that make your entire system more resilient. When you practice stress management, you switch on genes that help you handle future challenges. Your DNA isn't your destiny; it's your starting material, and you're the architect.

Steve Judge embodies this principle perfectly. When doctors told him he might never walk again after a car accident crushed both his legs, Steve could have chosen the victim's narrative. Instead, he chose self-authorship. Today, he is a two-time Paratriathlon World Champion.

"When I was told I may never walk again, that's where my goal setting came in," Steve told me. But his transformation wasn't about external goals but an internal identity shift from victim to champion.

"I used everything that happened to me before the accident, whether it was being fit and setting goals in sports, being an engineer, or being in scouting. Suddenly, I was now fighting for my life, trying to survive, setting that as a goal, and then setting minor goals throughout my rehabilitation, eventually growing my leg back, learning to stand again, and learning to walk again.

I got into swimming and cycling and eventually found Power Triathlon, a triathlon for disabled people. I became the British champion, set goals, became the European champion, set even further and bigger goals, and eventually became the world champion. In 2011 and 2012."

Steve is a goal-setter, and at first glance, it might appear he was setting external goals, but his journey to world champion was an internal transformation.

During his rehabilitation, Steve was introduced to this quote by Dan Sullivan.

"The definition of hell is: Your last day on Earth; the person you became meets the person you could have become"

The quote struck deeply because Steve realized he could become angry and bitter, focusing on what the accident had taken from him, or he could live a life without regrets.

Steve saw two possible futures and chose the one without regrets. As I discussed this with him, he said it was like receiving advice from his future self. This story clearly demonstrates the three pillars of self-leadership.

- **Self-Awareness:** Recognizing he had a choice between victim and champion narratives.
- **Self-Regulation:** Managing the emotional trauma and choosing constructive responses.
- **Self-Learning:** Using his engineering background and adapting his goal-setting skills to a new reality.

His genes didn't change, he didn't get a new pair of legs, but his response to his circumstances changed everything.

You might think, "That's an extraordinary situation, but what about everyday limitations that feel hardwired?"

Here's a fascinating example that shows how even our most basic preferences aren't as fixed as we think.

THE CURIOUS CASE OF BROCCOLI

Whether you love or hate broccoli might seem like a personal preference, but the effect of a gene (TAS2R38) programs some people to experience it as overwhelmingly bitter.

If you are a parent who's ever labeled your child a "picky eater" for refusing broccoli, they might be experiencing as punishment what tastes to you like a delightful snack. What I find interesting is that despite genetic predisposition, repeated exposure (10–15 times) can increase acceptance even among children genetically wired to taste bitterness. Watching their parents enjoy broccoli influences children to try it despite their taste sensitivity. Preparation methods can reduce bitter compounds, and positive reinforcement can overcome initial genetic aversion.

Studies show that genetic factors account for approximately 46% of food preferences, leaving substantial room for influence and modification.

The lesson? Your genes hand you the ingredients, but you choose the recipe. Just because you initially resist something – whether that be broccoli, public speaking, or learning to code – does not mean you can't develop a taste for it.

This insight about overcoming genetic predisposition isn't just modern science; it's ancient wisdom. Humans have always grappled with the question of whether we're

prisoners of our nature or masters of our destiny. Two and
a half thousand years ago, this same tension played out dramatically in Ancient Greece...

ANCIENT WISDOM FOR MODERN CHALLENGES

The Ancient Greeks experimented with two radically different approaches to human potential, and the tension still
shapes how we think about development today.

The Delphi approach taught "Know Thyself," the idea
that human potential flourishes when individuals understand and express their authentic nature. This philosophy
emphasizes personal growth, self-discovery, and individual
excellence.

The Spartan approach subordinated individual potential to collective needs. Spartans created a system where personal desires were entirely subservient to state objectives. It
produced magnificent warriors, but at the cost of individual
creativity and self-expression.

What's fascinating is that both approaches worked
within their contexts. Sparta produced legendary fighters
who held off vastly superior numbers at Thermopylae (as
lionized in the movie 300), while Athens produced philosophy, art, and democracy that still influence us today.

Which is better for potential?

1. Organizations that emphasize "bringing your whole self
   to work" encourage diverse perspectives and create space
   for individual expression and development.

2. Companies that hire for "cultural fit" implement standardized performance metrics and reward conformity to predetermined success models. Employees become interchangeable units optimized for specific functions.

The wisdom for our AI age lies not in choosing one approach over the other, but in integrating both insights: know yourself deeply enough to understand what you uniquely offer, then serve something larger than yourself that gives meaning and direction to your unique gifts.

STOICISM PRACTICES FOR MODERN SELF-LEADERSHIP

The Stoics, contemporaries of these Greek philosophers, discovered practical techniques that bridge individual development with service to something larger.

Over two thousand years ago, they discovered something that will guide you: life will test you, but you always get to choose your response. This isn't about becoming emotionless; it's about becoming unshakeable. Everything changes when you realize that your inner world is the one territory you truly govern.

Here are three updated Stoic practices that directly nurture self-leadership in our modern context.

1. **The Dichotomy of Control:** Continuously categorize every situation into "what's up to me" versus "what's not up to me." Focus your energy only on what you can influence. You can't control whether you get promoted, but

you can control your effort and skill development. You can't control others' responses, but you can control how you communicate.

2. **Morning Intention Setting:** Begin each day by setting intentions. "What kind of person do I want to be today?" "What challenges might I face, and how will I respond?" "What are the most important things I can positively influence today?" This builds self-regulation by visualizing how you will choose to think, feel, and act in the situations you encounter.

3. **Evening Review:** End each day by reviewing your actions, decisions, and reactions. Ask: "What did I do well today?" "Where did I fall short of my values?" "What can I learn?" This practice builds self-awareness faster than any other technique, creating a feedback loop between your intentions and actions.

Unfortunately, modern culture's "Stoic Bro" phenomenon has perverted the grounded practices of the Stoics, promoting a form of toxic masculinity. Social media platforms such as Instagram and TikTok are flooded with "Stoic quotes" overlaid with images of muscular men, luxury cars, and success imagery. These posts typically focus on emotional suppression ("don't let them see you hurt") rather than the Stoics' actual emphasis on rational virtue and service to others.

Don't be fooled by this "one-size-fits-all" prescription without a diagnosis approach. We are all different, and gender, age, personality, culture, and neurodivergence should be factored in when you plan to potentialize.

We are living through the most significant amplification of human capability in history. As the Stoics understood, how we respond to this transformation will determine whether it elevates us or overwhelms us.

Your Human Edge in an AI World

Here's why self-leadership matters more now than ever: as AI handles more routine cognitive tasks, the uniquely human capabilities become increasingly valuable. But these capabilities (emotional intelligence, creative problem-solving, the ability to inspire others) all depend on your ability to lead yourself first.

AI can process information, but it can't choose your attitude; it can optimize processes, but it can't decide your values; it can generate content, but only you determine your character.

I have found a perspective about AI that most people miss: AI is like a mirror with a megaphone. Whatever you bring to it – fear, wisdom, chaos, or clarity – gets amplified. If you are being reactive and scattered, AI can help you be reactive and scattered faster. But if you're grounded and intentional? AI becomes your superpower for expressing your authentic self.

The bus driver, Steve Judge, and the Stoics understood something profound: regardless of our circumstances or challenges, we can always exercise the power to choose our response. That choice and taking ownership of our actions, that practice of self-leadership, make us uniquely human.

This brings us to a crucial question: how do you develop internal stability to thrive in a world of exponential change? The answer lies in building what I like to call your self-leadership operating system.

BUILDING YOUR SELF-LEADERSHIP OPERATING SYSTEM

Self-leadership is not about becoming perfect or eliminating all negative emotions. It's about developing your "operating system," the fundamental processes determining how you interpret experiences, make decisions, and act.

Just as your computer's operating system runs in the background, enabling all other programs, your self-leadership operating system runs continuously, influencing every aspect of your performance and potential.

The most successful people I've coached over 25 years share this trait: they've developed robust self-leadership operating systems. They know themselves deeply, manage their emotional states skillfully, and learn from every experience. They don't avoid challenges. They use challenges to learn what they are capable of and then upgrade their inner software.

In the age of AI, this inner work becomes your competitive advantage. While machines can increasingly replicate human output, they cannot replicate human wisdom, compassion, or the quiet confidence that comes from knowing yourself and choosing your response to whatever life presents.

Being human is about experience. We will all have good, bad, and mundane experiences, such as falling in love, losing money, getting fired, and enjoying a meal with friends.

You can passively have these experiences or use your human agency to choose to uncover and unlock your potential and become your future self.

The foundation of unlocking your potential isn't found in the latest productivity hack or AI tool, though these can be valuable. It's found in the space between stimulus and response, and claiming authorship of your inner world. When you can lead effectively, you unleash your potential and inspire others to excel.

Potential is, therefore, the "why" of self-leadership.

In 2017, I had the pleasure of interviewing the legendary author and motivator Brian Tracy about his view on self-leadership:

> *"Self-leadership is the starting point of everything. Self-leadership means that you decide exactly who you are and what you want, and then you write it down, and you make a plan and a goal, and you work on it every day. And especially, self-leadership means you accept complete responsibility for your results and outcomes; you don't blame other people, you don't make excuses, you say, 'I am responsible,' I'm in control, I'm in charge of my own life"*

We will not achieve our purpose or potential unless we take responsibility and operate as a conscious agent.

TRY THIS: SHIFT FROM PASSENGER TO DRIVER

The journey from passenger to driver begins with understanding that your "self" is more fluid and changeable than you might think. This exercise helps you take the wheel of your own story using the IGNITE framework.

INSPIRE – AUTHORING YOUR STORY

Passenger Versus Driver Assessment

Rate each statement from 1 (never) to 5 (always):

- I make decisions based on my values rather than others' expectations ____
- When something goes wrong, I focus on what I can control ____
- I actively shape my circumstances rather than react to them ____
- I take responsibility for my outcomes without blaming others ____

Total Score: ____/20 (16+ = Driver mode, 12–15 = Mixed, under 12 = Passenger mode)

GUIDE – YOUR INNER GUIDANCE SYSTEM

Stoic Practice Integration

For the next week, practice these daily check-ins.

Morning Intention: "Today I will focus my energy only on what I can control, which includes. . ."

Evening Review

- When did I respond from choice rather than reaction?
- What triggered my reactive patterns?
- What am I learning about my capacity to lead myself?

Write down your commitment to this practice: "I will practice self-leadership by. . ."

Nurture – Embracing Your Fluid Self

Your DNA Isn't Your Destiny

Identify one "limitation" you've always accepted about yourself.

- Is this truly genetic/unchangeable, or a story you've been told?
- What would be possible if this weren't fixed?
- What's one small way you could test this assumption this week?

Example: "I'm not creative" → "I haven't found my creative medium yet"

Take the Wheel

That bus driver in Sydney understood something most people miss: leadership isn't about the authority you're given, it's about the responsibility you take. In the next chapter, we'll explore how this internal foundation enables you to inspire others and unlock potential you didn't know existed. But first, you must take the wheel of your own life.

The question isn't whether you have potential. The question is, will you drive it, or let it drive you?

It's time to wake up from the fog and reclaim your power.

CHAPTER 3

THE PASSION CONFUSION: WHY COMPETENCE COMES FIRST

"Follow your passion is advice for people who already have money"

– Mark Cuban

Have you ever noticed that the most passionate people often struggle the most? They chase dreams with fervor but lack the skills to execute them, while AI quietly masters the very capabilities they wish they had. It is likely that, at one time or another, you have been told to "follow your passion," either directly by a mentor or indirectly through a motivational poster or meme.

This advice feels even more dangerous now that AI can execute many passion projects faster and cheaper than humans ever could. While people wait for their passion to reveal itself, AI is quietly making their imagined dream jobs obsolete. The question isn't whether you're passionate enough; it's whether you're capable enough to partner with machines rather than be replaced by them.

Thought-leader, psychologist, and Stanford University professor Carol Dweck observes, "Potential without passion risks remaining dormant. It's the emotional engine of passion that transforms potential into achievement." But what if we have been telling the story backward?

What might surprise you is that most climbers didn't start out "passionate" about mountaineering. They developed that passion through competence, achievement, and the intoxicating drug of mastery.

If you want to potentialize, it's time to flip the script on passion.

THE MYTH THAT'S KILLING POTENTIAL

This seemingly inspirational advice can destroy human potential. Passion without competence creates frustration. Passion without identifying a market need creates poverty. Passion without persistence creates abandonment.

Because I am relatively well known as a global keynote speaker, I regularly get calls from aspiring speakers wanting to know my "secret." The call typically starts with them saying, "I am passionate about topic X, how can I get booked internationally?"

I explain this with as much tact as I can muster: AI can now generate compelling presentations on virtually any topic in minutes. Event organizers aren't looking for passionate speakers; they are looking for speakers with deep competence who can offer insights that no algorithm can replicate. That requires the kind of insight and wisdom that only comes from systematic skill development and real-world application.

It's good to be excited about your idea; this can ignite your search for answers and insight into a topic. In the words of Pablo Picasso: "Learn the rules like a pro so that you can break them like an artist."

The passion-first mythology isn't just wrong; it's dangerous. But the alternative isn't passion-free drudgery. It's something far more reliable: building passion through the systematic development of competence.

This principle works across every domain I've studied, from boardrooms to weight rooms.

THE COMPETENCE-CREATES-PASSION REVELATION

Entrepreneur Ben Horowitz cuts through this passion mythology with characteristic Silicon Valley directness: "Successful people say they love what they do, so the common belief is that passion leads to success. But what if success creates passion?"

This isn't cynical, it's liberating. It means you don't need to wait for a "road-to-Damascus" moment. You can build passion through a more reliable path: competence.

Horowitz said this in his commencement speech to the Columbia University class of 2015: "Passions are tricky. But figuring out what you're good at? That's much easier."

- Studies show that passion emerges after thousands of hours of deliberate practice.
- People become passionate about activities they are good at, not activities they initially loved.
- Competence creates confidence, confidence creates engagement, and engagement creates passion.
- The feeling of mastery releases dopamine and creates intrinsic motivation.

I spent years believing I wasn't creative because my sister was the "artist" in the family, and I couldn't draw beyond stick figures. The passion wasn't there. But then I started writing and speaking professionally, not because I was passionate about it, but because I needed to develop these skills. Something unexpected happened; as people began to share with me how my message and methodologies had inspired and equipped them to lead themselves, creative potential I never knew existed began to emerge. Not because I was passionate about writing, but because I was willing to develop competence in it.

Today, I am passionate about helping others unlock their potential. But that passion emerged from competence, not the other way around.

Instead of asking "What am I passionate about?" ask:

- What could I become genuinely skilled at?
- Where could I make a meaningful contribution?
- What challenges would force me to grow?
- How could AI amplify rather than replace these capabilities?

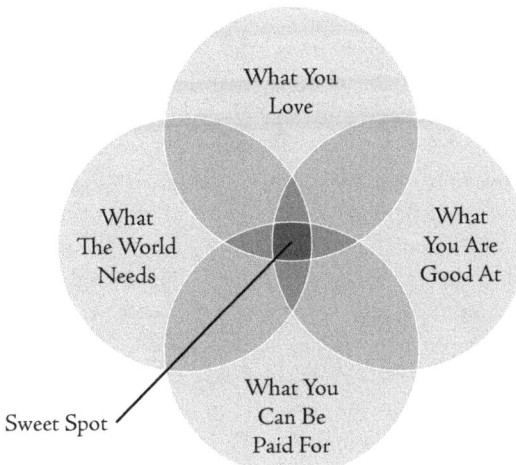

Figure 3.1   The Ikigai Sweet Spot

The Japanese call this sweet spot your *Ikigai.* See Figure 3.1.

Look for your sweet spot, the intersection between your natural talent, market demand, what you enjoy, and what the world needs. But add a fifth circle to the traditional Ikigai model: what AI can amplify rather than replace. The Japanese concept becomes even more powerful when you ask not just "What can I be paid for?" but also "What can I become exceptionally good at that becomes more valuable when combined with AI?"

Formula One champion Ayrton Senna's journey perfectly illustrates this progression. He didn't start out passionate about inspiring others but about pure speed. Listen to how his purpose evolved after two decades of relentless skill development.

"I'm a racing driver. I think that even before I got into a car, I already knew I was born to race. Since I was a boy, I had this feeling that the world moved too slow for me. It was like I had a different perception of everything. Of time, especially. My mother says I didn't learn to walk. I learned to race. She called me 'Little Volcano.' Then one day, I got into the go-kart that Milton, my dad, built for me. And that's when I found myself, for real. It was just me, the car, and the track. Just me and time. That's it. I'm a racing driver. And, for a driver, the battle is always against time but never just against time. It's an endless joy. It's adventure, adrenaline. Pure racing. When I was a boy, I only wanted to race and win for myself. I think that after 20 years of racing, I learned that no one wins alone. That's why I never stopped racing. Because when I'm in my car, I know that I'm not alone."

Notice the progression: individual passion ("I only wanted to race and win for myself") transformed into something larger ("no one wins alone") through sustained competence development. This is the competence-creates-purpose pathway that passion-first advice completely misses.

Senna's evolution from self-focused to purpose-driven excellence through competence development isn't unique to Formula One champions. Sometimes this journey begins in the most unexpected circumstances, as I discovered when I met Adhisha Dahanayake from Sri Lanka.

FROM GRIEF TO GOLD: THE ACCIDENTAL POWERLIFTER

Adhisha Dahanayake co-founded Double XL, an inclusive fashion brand, and is a national champion powerlifter.

When Adhisha's father died, she wasn't passionate about powerlifting. She was a grieving entrepreneur looking for any outlet to help her heal. She tried everything: partying with friends, traveling through Europe, and attending yoga retreats in Melbourne and Brussels. Nothing worked.

She returned home and told her personal trainer, "Listen, this time I don't want to lose weight, I just want to focus and get fitter and stronger."

She wasn't drawn to lifting weights by passion but by necessity. She needed an outlet to process her grief and rebuild her confidence.

While working out at her gym, she was spotted by Darin Weerasinghe, a Sri Lankan powerlifting champion and Commonwealth gold medalist. Seeing her pulling weights, Darin invited her to join the team. Adhisha said yes, not because she loved the sport, but because she was "looking for an outlet" and wanted to "bring that focus back."

What happened next perfectly illustrates the competence-first principle: she developed competence systematically. She trained consistently. At her first competition, she lifted 62.5 kg and set a national record in Sri Lanka. Only then did her mindset shift: "I felt like, okay, I should invest in this."

Adhisha won gold in 2021 at the Sri Lankan National Powerlifting Competition. In the under-84 kg class, she lifted a total of 322.5 kg.

Adhisha says powerlifting was "one of the best decisions I have ever made in my life." Today, Adhisha uses fitness apps and AI-powered training programs, but her passion for the sport came from the irreplaceable human experience of pushing through barriers and discovering capabilities she didn't know existed.

Adhisha's transformation reveals something crucial about sustainable motivation. But what happens when you have already achieved success through one type of drive?

One of my coaching clients discovered this challenge firsthand. My client, Shantanu Verma, who runs a marketing agency, recently called me to discuss a slump in his motivation: "I struggle to get out of bed in the morning," he told me. "I used to leap up at 5 a.m., excited to hustle. Now I hit the snooze button three times and drag myself to the office."

This wasn't depression; his business was thriving, his team was growing, and his clients were happy. But something had shifted.

When his agency was struggling and money was tight, every morning brought clear urgency: make calls, find clients, survive another day. That fear-driven energy had fueled years of 12-hour days. But success had eliminated the external pressure masquerading as passion. "I thought I was passionate about marketing," Shantanu reflected. "But I was really just passionate about not being broke."

As we worked together, we discovered that Shantanu had built genuine competence in digital marketing, client relationship management, and team leadership. His technical skills were strong, his agency was profitable, but he'd never connected his competence to a larger purpose.

The breakthrough came when Shantanu realized his marketing competence could serve something larger than survival: it could help small businesses compete globally while giving him the freedom to design his ideal lifestyle.

Within days, his motivation had returned because his competence now served a purpose worthy of his skills.

Shantanu's journey reveals something crucial: even when we've built competence successfully, we can still lose direction if that competence isn't connected to what we truly value.

My own experience, and stories like Senna's, Adhisha's, and Shantanu's, taught me that the competence-first approach requires a structured approach to be sustainable. You can't just build skills randomly and hope passion emerges. You need a systematic way to develop competence that naturally evolves into purpose. That's exactly what the IGNITE framework provides: a roadmap for transforming competence into lasting passion and meaningful contribution.

THE IGNITE FRAMEWORK APPLIED TO COMPETENCE

This competence-first approach aligns perfectly with the IGNITE framework for potential development. Let me show you how each element supports building passion through capability.

INSPIRE through contribution, not passion-chasing. Instead of waiting for inspiration, inspire others through your growing competence and contribution. The bus driver who inspired me wasn't passionate about public transportation; he was competent at creating positive experiences for others – something no algorithm could replicate.

GUIDE toward skill development, not dream pursuit. Seek mentors who can guide your chosen competence development, not cheerleaders for your passions. Find people who've walked the path of systematic skill-building.

NURTURE growth mindset, not passion dependency. Surround yourself with others committed to competence development. Belong to communities that value growth over feeling.

INTEGRATE AI to amplify competence. Use AI as your practice partner and capability multiplier, not your replacement. Let it accelerate your skill-building while you focus on uniquely human applications and wisdom development.

TRANSFORM through challenge, not comfort. Choose challenges that force competence development, even when they don't feel passionate. Embrace the discomfort of being a beginner.

EVALUATE contribution and growth, not passion levels. Measure your progress in skills gained, problems solved, and people helped, not how passionate you feel.

TRY THIS: THE COMPETENCE-FIRST AUDIT

Week 1: Skill Identification

1. List three skills you could develop that are:
   - Valuable to others
   - Difficult for AI to replicate

- Buildable through practice
- Connected to problems you care about solving

2. For each skill, ask: What would basic competence look like? What would mastery look like?

Week 2: Competence Baseline

1. Assess your current level in each skill (1–10 scale)
2. Identify one specific way to practice each skill this week
3. Use AI tools to accelerate your learning (research, practice, feedback)

Week 3: Contribution Connection

1. Find one way to use your developing skills to help someone else
2. Notice how serving others affects your engagement with skill-building
3. Track competence growth, not passion levels

Week 4: Passion Tracking

1. Notice if your engagement with these skills has changed
2. Observe any emerging passion or interest
3. Reflect: What's creating this engagement – the feeling or the competence?

The Competence Revolution

We can continue chasing the passion myth, waiting for an aha moment, while AI makes our desired work obsolete. Or we can embrace the competence-first revolution, systematically building the capabilities that will make us irreplaceable partners with AI.

The choice isn't between passion and competence; it's between passion as a starting point and passion as a destination. When you build competence first, passion follows. When you contribute meaningfully, engagement deepens. When you grow through challenges, fulfillment emerges.

Adhisha Dahanayake wasn't initially passionate about powerlifting. She started grieving and looking for focus. However, through systematic competence development, she built not just strength, but passion – enough to become a champion.

This is how you unlock potential in the age of AI: not by following your passion, but by building competence that creates passion while partnering strategically with AI. Your journey begins with the first rep, the first practice session, the first attempt at something you're not yet good at. AI can guide your form and track your progress, but only you can experience the transformation that turns competence into passion.

CHAPTER 4

RIDING THE DRAGON

"The cave you fear to enter holds the treasure you seek"

– Joseph Campbell

So far in this book, I have made the case for self-leadership and for developing competence that creates lasting passion. But what happens when you actually try to develop new capabilities in an AI world? What happens when that voice in your head whispers, "Why bother learning this when a machine can do it better?"

This is where most people get stuck. They understand the competence-first principle but struggle to overcome the resistance that emerges when they actually start building those capabilities.

The paradox is that we carry the power of a supercomputer in our phones yet make decisions with ancient fears. We have godlike technological power, but caveman emotional responses to change.

Despite how sophisticated we might feel with our fancy clothes and our high-speed internet, deep down in the darkest places of our psyche, there are things we fear and our inner genius that we must learn to trust. We must face our dragons; learning to ride them is essential for potentializing in the AI age. Dragons appear in every culture not because they're real, but because they represent something universal: the thing we fear the most often guards what we need the most.

Western psychologists, such as Jung, considered "dragons" to be things we repress; in contrast, Chinese mythological dragons embody beneficial powers associated with water, rainfall, and abundance.

To be fully human, we must integrate these unconscious forces rather than bury them.

If we fear AI, it will become a dragon, but if we reframe it as a partner, we can learn to dance with it.

When I first encountered AI writing tools, my immediate reaction was territorial. "This is my expertise! How dare a machine try to correct my grammar or give feedback on my content structure!" That's classic dragon-fighting behavior. But then I realized: what if AI could help me research faster, organize my thoughts more clearly, and explore angles I hadn't considered?

Now I use AI as my research partner, thought-sparring partner, and editor. It helps me process information and generate initial frameworks, but my lived experience, client stories, and hard-won wisdom are what transform AI-generated concepts into insights that actually help people. The dragon didn't replace my expertise; it amplified my ability to share it. As we saw in Chapter 2, our sense of self is fluid and constructed from our identity and stories. These, in turn, are influenced by feelings and memories from our body and culture.

Therefore, we can "tame" our dragons and potentialize by understanding where they have come from and how they have been constructed.

Consider the successful professional who achieves everything on paper yet battles internal anxiety. Despite career advancement and external validation, they experience presentation anxiety and feelings of being an impostor, resulting in severe stress. This "dragon" pattern reveals how success can mask rather than resolve our deepest fears.

The breakthrough comes not from eliminating fear but from understanding its protective intention, transforming the internal saboteur into an ally. Instead of suppressing the fear, we can ask: "What do you call this anxiety?" "Where do you think it comes from?" "What do you think its positive intention is?" "What if what you are feeling is preparation, not panic?"

In other words, the voice in your head can either be your greatest ally or your worst enemy. Internal dialogue significantly impacts confidence, performance, and the ability to lead ourselves and others.

AI AS THE DRAGON

When futurist Brooks Cole told me he viewed collaborating with AI as "Riding the Dragon," I knew I had found a kindred spirit, and he had found the perfect metaphor.

AI isn't the sci-fi villain we feared. Instead, it is a mirror, reflecting our collective knowledge, creativity, and, yes, our biases back to us, amplified and accelerated.

Think about it: AI is trained on our collective knowledge, creativity, and expression. It is essentially humanity's greatest hits album, except it includes all the B-sides we would rather forget.

Like our mental dragons, AI forces us to confront both our light and shadow sides.

Stephen Hawking warned that AI could be "the biggest event in human history. . . unfortunately, it might also be the last." But what if the real danger isn't AI becoming too smart, but us behaving like cavemen, afraid of our own shadows?

WHAT ARE WE GETTING WRONG?

I spoke with Steve Cadigan, LinkedIn's first Chief HR Officer and now a Silicon Valley talent strategist: "What I think we're getting wrong about AI is that this is more of a cultural challenge than a technical challenge. This is more about us having to confront our own insecurities. Like if someone says, 'Hey Steve, go see what you can do with AI,' I'm like, 'why would I do that? It's going to make me less valuable.'"

This is an excellent example of the dragon manifesting as negative self-talk.

REFRAMING THE DRAGONS OF SELF-TALK ABOUT AI AND TECHNOLOGY

With self-awareness, we can catch our internal dialogue and EVALUATE it to see if it empowers us to move toward our objectives. Negative self-talk can be reframed for us to be more effective. See Figure 4.1.

Negative Self-Talk	Reframed Narrative
AI is going to take my job. I'll become obsolete. There's no point in developing my skills because machines will do everything better than me.	AI is a tool that can enhance my capabilities, not replace my human judgment and creativity. I can learn to work alongside AI to become more effective and valuable. My ability to think critically, build relationships, and solve complex problems remains uniquely human.
I don't understand AI or technology well enough. Everyone else seems to get it, but I'm too old/inexperienced/non-technical to learn. I'll be left behind.	I don't need to be an AI engineer to benefit from AI tools. I can learn to use AI applications at my own pace, just like I learned to use email, smartphones, and other technologies. My domain expertise combined with AI tools can create powerful results.
If I use AI to help with my work, I'm cheating. People will think I'm not really capable. My contributions won't be genuine or valuable anymore.	Using AI is like using a calculator, it's about working smarter, not cheating. My judgment in directing AI, interpreting results, and applying insights is where my value lies. I can be transparent about my tools while taking credit for my strategic thinking.

(continued)

(continued)

Negative Self-Talk	Reframed Narrative
AI can write better than me, design better than me, and develop more creative ideas. What's the point of my creative work if a machine can do it faster and better?	AI generates content based on patterns from existing work, but I bring lived experience, emotional intelligence, and unique perspective that no machine can replicate. I can use AI as a creative collaborator to enhance and accelerate my ideas, not replace my vision.

Figure 4.1   Reframing Negative AI Self-Talk

- Do you see the reframing pattern in these examples?
- Your "dragons" (fears) are actually trying to protect you, but what if you no longer need protection?

Understanding AI as a dragon we can learn to ride is the first step. But to climb on the dragon's back and ride it like a pro, we need precise awareness of our own capabilities and readiness. If only there were a way to know...

YOUR INTERNAL GPS: NAVIGATING POTENTIAL WITH PRECISION

"That wasn't flying, it was falling with style"
— *Woody to Buzz in* **Toy Story**

Most development "advice" frustrates me because it's like being told to "drive better" without knowing where you are, or the road conditions. You can't improve what you can't feel or develop what you can't locate.

Athletes have a built-in advantage here. A gymnast knows precisely where their body is in space. This sense of position and movement is called proprioception. Without it, gymnasts would crash into the mat every time.

But what about your potential? Do you have the same precise awareness of where you stand with your capabilities, growth, and opportunities? Most people are flying blind.

That's when I realized: if gymnasts need proprioception for their bodies, maybe we need something similar for our potential. Not some fluffy self-awareness exercise, but a precise diagnostic tool.

As a former physiotherapist, I've seen what happens when someone loses proprioception. They can't walk straight, judge distances, or coordinate movement. When you watch an expert rider on a horse in dressage or directing cattle in a rodeo, you witness human and animal's proprioceptive synergy.

To develop that kind of synergy for riding the AI dragon, we need what athletes have always had: precise awareness of where we stand and where we're going.

Let me introduce you to the Potential Proprioception model. See Figure 4.2.

Think of this model as your personal GPS and dashboard. Instead of wondering "Am I growing?" or "Where should I focus?" you'll know precisely where you stand across six critical dimensions.

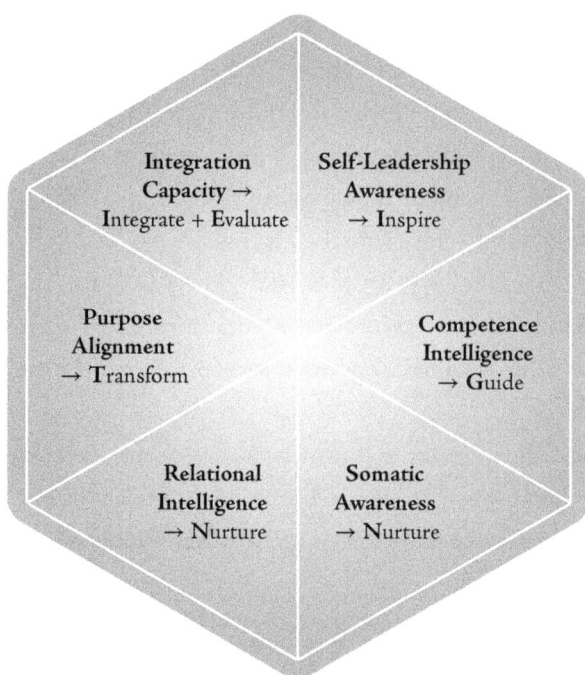

Figure 4.2   The Potential Proprioception Model

DON'T PANIC: I am not introducing another model; you will recognize the elements of the IGNITE framework. See Figure 4.3.

Here's how it works step by step.

STEP 1: UNDERSTAND THE SIX DIMENSIONS

Your potential exists across six interconnected areas, like instruments on a pilot's dashboard. Each one gives you different but essential information.

1. **Self-Leadership Awareness:** Are you the author of your story or living someone else's script?

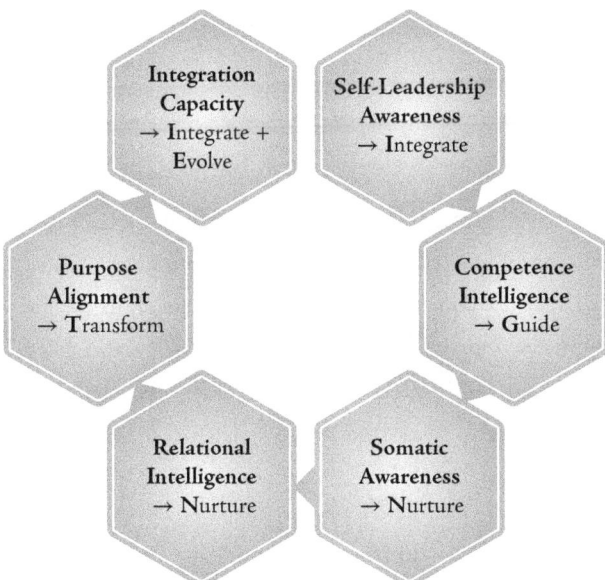

Figure 4.3   Potential Proprioception + IGNITE

2. **Competence Intelligence:** What can you do well, and where are you growing?
3. **Somatic Awareness:** How does your body and energy support or limit your potential?
4. **Relational Intelligence:** How do you show up in relationships and communities?
5. **Purpose Alignment:** Is your daily work connected to your deeper sense of meaning?
6. **Integration Capacity:** How effectively are you combining the available technologies and wisdom with your human strengths?

STEP 2: TAKE YOUR READINGS

For each dimension, you'll rate yourself on a scale of 1–10. But here's the key: this isn't about being "good" or "bad."

It's about being accurate. A pilot needs to know their actual altitude, not their desired altitude.

Step 3: Look for Patterns

Once you have your six readings, patterns emerge. Maybe your purpose alignment is high, but your competence intelligence is low. That tells you something specific: you know what matters to you, but you need to build skills to get there. Perhaps your self-leadership awareness is strong, but your relational intelligence lags. You understand yourself well, but struggle to read others.

Step 4: Choose Your Development Focus

Instead of trying to improve everything at once (which leads nowhere), you pick the dimension that's most limiting your progress right now. Usually, it's your lowest score, but not always. Sometimes, a slight improvement in one area unlocks massive progress everywhere else.

Step 5: Recalibrate Regularly

Like any navigation system, Potential Proprioception works best when updated regularly. As you grow and change, your readings will shift. What was once your weakest area might become your strength.

Why This Matters

You can't reach your potential if you don't know your own capabilities and blind spots. Potential Proprioception is your flight training before you climb on the dragon's back.

The model tracks six interconnected areas that align with the IGNITE framework we've been working with.

Don't worry about memorizing them. We'll explore each one throughout this book. For now, notice how they connect to everything we've discussed about self-leadership, competence-first development, and riding the AI dragon.

Now, let me show you how this model helped someone navigate and saved their life.

THE TWO WITNESSES: WHEN POTENTIAL PROPRIOCEPTION SAVED A LIFE

Marina Traub, a competitive rower turned yoga teacher, learned about the power of awareness the hard way. For years, she had been what she calls "a typical nut job," pushing through exhaustion, ignoring her body's signals, and measuring her worth entirely through external achievement. Her stock in trade was her ability to ignore how she felt and press on anyway.

"I grew up in New England's sufferer culture," she told me. "If it didn't hurt, it wasn't worth anything. The harder you work, the more you're worth. Anything that didn't cost you everything must not be worth anything."

This worked until it nearly killed her potential entirely.

Marina described the moment when her internal GPS finally broke through the noise: "I eventually surrendered. I can no longer pretend not to know what I know, which is that I am living out of alignment with my values."

She had discovered what Buddhist philosophy calls "the two witnesses." In any moment, there's a voice measuring and comparing everything relative to past experiences. But there's also what she calls "the beginner's mind that's just there experiencing it as if for the first time."

"The friction and the tension of living in conflict with yourself is what tires us out," Marina explained. "It's what drains us of our potency and potential."

Her breakthrough came when she learned to check in with her Potential Proprioception across all dimensions.

Self-Leadership Awareness: She stopped pretending she didn't know she was exhausted and misaligned.

Somatic Awareness: She began asking, "Where in my body do I feel this?" instead of pushing through physical signals.

Relational Intelligence: She recognized that her need to prove herself was actually pushing people away.

Purpose Alignment: She admitted she was living someone else's definition of success, not her own.

Competence Intelligence: She shifted from measuring herself against others to developing her authentic capabilities.

Integration Capacity: She learned to combine ancient wisdom practices with modern life instead of compartmentalizing them.

The result wasn't instant transformation but what she calls "dandelion spores moments," when the small, fearful self dissolves and potential can emerge naturally.

"When I think of potential," Marina reflects, "I think of being connected to the part of you that just is. When that little tiny whiny part of me that's still scared and doesn't trust the world gets quiet, I can speak from somewhere other than her. That is me at my greatest potential."

This is Potential Proprioception in action: the precise awareness of where you are across all dimensions of your development and the wisdom to know which witness to listen to. Like Marina discovered, you can't develop what you can't sense, and you can't sense what you refuse to acknowledge.

Marina's story is about integrating ancient wisdom with modern life rather than the latest AI tools, but it is no less valid in making the point that we need to develop our awareness of both our internal and external worlds.

TRY THIS: LEARN TO RIDE YOUR DRAGON

In this chapter, AI is framed as the dragon – unpredictable, powerful, and potentially transformative. This exercise will help you turn that perceived threat into a partner for progress.

NAME YOUR DRAGON

Identify the AI, technology, or change you feel most overwhelmed or uncertain about.

"The dragon I'm facing right now is _____."

Now explore:

- What fear or resistance does this trigger in me?
- Is that fear based on loss of control, identity, or relevance?

FIND THE HIDDEN OPPORTUNITY

Complete this sentence:

"If I could collaborate with this 'dragon' instead of fearing it, I could _____."

Now, list one way this challenge or tool could actually *amplify* your creativity, productivity, or sense of purpose.

Example: "Using AI to automate routine tasks would free up time for deep strategy or mentoring others."

CHECK YOUR POTENTIAL PROPRIOCEPTION

Now that you've identified your dragon and potential opportunity, use these questions to assess your readiness to ride it. Rate yourself 1–5 on each dimension, then include the six key questions, one per dimension.

Self-Leadership: "Am I the author of my story or living someone else's script?"

Competence: "What can I do well, and where am I growing?"

Somatic: "How does my body/energy support or limit my potential?"

Relational: "How do I show up in relationships and communities?"

Purpose: "Is my daily work connected to my deeper sense of meaning?"

Integration: "How effectively am I combining existing wisdom and AI tools with my human judgment?"

Which dimension scored lowest? That's where to focus your dragon-riding preparation.

You have learned to name your dragons and find the hidden opportunities in technological change. You've discovered your internal GPS through Potential Proprioception, giving you precise awareness of where you stand across six critical dimensions of development, now it's time to extend your genius.

RIDING THE DRAGON: EXTENDING YOUR GENIUS

The dragon you refuse to ride will eventually ride you

The Ancient Romans believed everyone had a "genius" – not intelligence, but a guiding spirit that helped them discover their purpose. Modern AI can work like that genius, helping us see patterns and possibilities we might miss. As philosopher Andy Clark suggests, our minds already extend beyond our biological boundaries every time we write a note or set a phone reminder. AI represents the next frontier of this cognitive extension.

The key is intentionality. When embraced purposefully, AI becomes an extension of your cognitive architecture rather than a replacement for human judgment. Your unique genius remains irreplaceable. AI simply amplifies your capacity to express it.

But here's what separates those who successfully ride the dragon from those who get burned: they approach transformation from neither arrogant certainty nor crippling self-doubt. Both extremes sabotage potential.

Since overcoming my initial resistance to using AI as a creative partner in my writing projects, I continue to find new ways to unleash my potential.

Marina Traub discovered something profound during her transformation. She has identified both the voice that measures and compares, and the beginner's mind that experiences everything fresh. Her breakthrough came from knowing which voice to listen to in each moment.

This wisdom reveals something crucial about unlocking potential in the AI age. Success requires finding the sweet spot between absolute confidence and paralyzing uncertainty. It demands what I call "confident humility" – being sure of your abilities while remaining curious about what you don't yet know.

You now have the foundation. You understand why potential matters more than ever in an AI world. You've learned that self-leadership is your starting point, that competence creates lasting passion, and that AI is your dragon to ride, not your enemy to fight. You've discovered your internal GPS through Potential Proprioception, giving you precise awareness of where you stand across six critical dimensions of development.

But knowledge without action is just sophisticated procrastination. The gap between knowing and doing is where most potential dies. I've worked with countless leaders who could explain these concepts perfectly but struggled to implement them consistently. The difference between those who succeeded and those who stayed stuck wasn't intelligence or resources. It was their willingness to develop the specific capabilities that bridge understanding and implementation.

In Part II, we move from foundation to practice. You'll discover how to cultivate the confident humility that allows bold action while staying curious. You'll learn to reignite the curiosity and creativity that AI can amplify but never replace. Most importantly, you'll develop the resilience that transforms setbacks into comebacks, all while partnering strategically with AI.

The dragon is waiting. Your journey to maximizing potential begins now.

PART II

How To Maximize Potential?

The Practice

The gap between knowing and doing is where most potential dies.

In martial arts, the distinction is between knowing the forms and embodying them. A novice can memorize every movement, but a master has practiced until the techniques become second nature. The difference isn't knowledge; it's integration through deliberate practice.

The same principle applies to potential. You can understand every framework, recognize every pattern, and analyze every case study. However, your potential remains theoretical until you develop the specific capabilities that allow you to act on that understanding.

Part II is where theory becomes practice, concepts become capabilities, and potential becomes performance.

But this isn't practice for practice's sake. The capabilities you'll develop here will become more valuable as AI becomes more powerful. While AI handles routine cognitive tasks, you'll strengthen the distinctly human abilities that no algorithm can replicate.

You'll discover how to maintain confident humility and to partner with AI to amplify your natural curiosity and creativity rather than being intimidated by its capabilities. Most importantly, you will develop the psychological resilience that turns inevitable setbacks into accelerated growth.

Think of these as your core competencies for the intelligence age. Just as industrial workers needed to master machinery, and knowledge workers needed to master information systems, you must master the art of human–AI collaboration while staying authentically human.

Your practice begins now.

"The most important investment you can make is in yourself."
– Warren Buffet

CHAPTER 5

THE SWEET SPOT BETWEEN DOUBT AND DELUSION

"Once we believe in ourselves, we can risk curiosity, wonder, spontaneous delight, or any experience that reveals the human spirit"

– E.E. Cummings

Learning to ride the dragon requires a delicate balance. Too much confidence, and you'll get burned by arrogance. Too little, and you'll never climb on its back. The sweet spot between these extremes, what I call confident humility, is perhaps the most crucial skill for potentializing in the AI age.

But here's what I discovered the hard way: confident humility isn't just about finding balance within yourself. It's about understanding how that balance is perceived and received by others. When I moved from Sydney to Singapore in 2004, I learned this lesson in the most humbling way possible.

CONFIDENT HUMILITY

"You'd better learn to be humble, he said.

"How arrogant do you think I am?" was my defensive response.

"You are not arrogant," he replied carefully, "But confidence can look like arrogance when you don't understand the local rules of humility."

His words were prophetic. Within weeks, I was speaking when it wasn't my turn, challenging long-held beliefs without first establishing relationships. Not surprisingly, I met with polite but firm resistance.

I had confused directness with leadership and mistaken my British-Australian communication style for universal confidence.

What I learned in those early months in Singapore's multicultural business environment changed everything I thought I knew about leadership. The same behavior that had been viewed as confident leadership in Australia was being interpreted as disrespectful arrogance in Asia. It also reinforced the INSPIRE element of potentializing: authentic confidence comes not from being right, but from being curious enough to understand the context you're operating in.

In *The New Leadership Playbook* (Bryant, 2021), I wrote: "Confidence is not walking into a room thinking you are better than anybody else, confidence is walking into a room knowing you don't have to compare yourself to anyone else."

Confidence is the mindset of being sure of your abilities or having trust in people, plans, or the future. This is very different from arrogance, which is thinking your opinion is the most important and looking down on others.

Authentic confidence is grounded in competence and not driven by the ego's need to prove itself.

The word "humility" comes from the Latin *humilitas*, which translates as humble, but also as grounded or "from the earth," since it derives from humus (earth). The original concept of humility addresses intrinsic self-worth, relationships, socialization, and perspective.

I believe that self-regulating to a state of confident humility is the most effective way to potentialize. People lacking the confidence to speak up or try new things lose a vast amount of potential, and immeasurable harm has been done by those behaving with "arrogant certainty" without the critical thinking or capability to back it up.

Self-awareness about our intentions, values, beliefs, and narratives allows us to self-regulate a state of confident humility. This means appreciating our competencies and all the other resources we have access to. These resources include our friends, family, and even AI agents. We do not have to enter a room alone; we take our resources with us.

A state of confident humility does not mean we know everything; instead, we are grounded in the knowledge that if we don't know something, we can find out and learn it.

In the age of AI, confident humility has become essential for human–machine collaboration. You need enough confidence to contribute unique human insights while remaining humble enough to learn from AI capabilities you don't yet understand.

A state of confident humility comes with curiosity; curiosity about what others are going through. What are their needs, wants, and beliefs? This curiosity sets you up for collaboration rather than competition, but first, we must face the impostor.

Confronting the Impostor

Impostor syndrome is a psychological pattern that involves doubting one's skills and being fearful of being exposed. It is usually experienced by high-performing individuals who compare themselves negatively with other high-performers.

We can confront the impostor and potentialize by developing self-awareness and revealing our dragons. Once we know our potential, we can safely reveal it to others. See Figure 5.1.

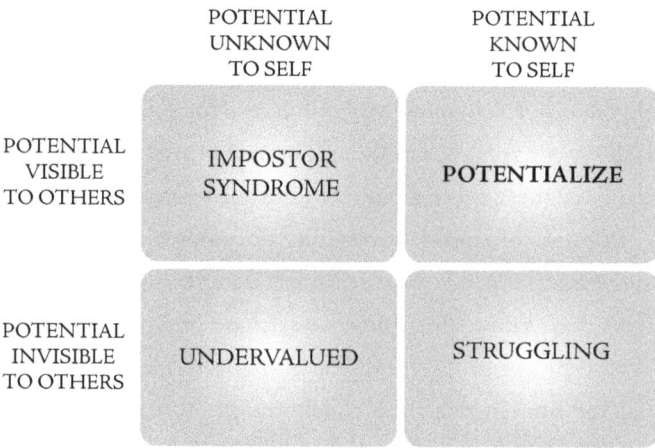

Figure 5.1   Impostor to Potential

- If we know our potential, but it is invisible to others, we will struggle to be successful.
- If we don't know or undervalue our potential by comparing ourselves negatively to others, we can suffer from impostor syndrome.
- If our potential is not visible to ourselves or others, we will be undervalued and fail to potentialize.

With many years of coaching experience, I am adept at listening to the frames of mind that inhibit potential. Recently, I listened to a woman tell me about her situation, and my mind conjured up an image of her in a room with a door, but she didn't know that the door existed. The room was constructed from her culture's expectations and the limitations she had placed on how far she could progress in her career. In Chapter 2, we explored how the illusion of self is constructed and how culture can influence memories, influencing our stories.

"What if I told you there was a door to escape your current situation?" I asked her."And what if you can't see the door because you don't have a big enough reason to go through it?"

I spoke with Dr. Marcia Reynolds, one of the world's most respected coaches, about potential, and she reinforced the need to answer why we need to find the door.

"We rarely define what we want our future, our destination, to look like. What do we see when we will be able to say I've reached my potential."

"Who are you?" I ask my clients, "What do you really want to have or change? What does that look like in your life?" And I say, "So, who are you in that picture?" I have to ask the question at least three times because they tell me what they're doing.

I say, "No, I didn't ask you what you're doing. I'm asking, who are you being?" And it's such a difficult question because they don't have an orientation to that.

Remember the Potential Proprioception model from Chapter 4? Just as elite athletes develop exquisite body awareness to perform at their peak, overcoming impostor syndrome requires precise awareness of your capabilities, position, and destination.

When impostor feelings arise, use these proprioceptive check-ins.

Self-Leadership Awareness: "Am I comparing my internal experience to others' external performance? What story am I telling myself right now?"

Competence Intelligence: "What can I do well right now? What specific evidence supports my capabilities?" This isn't about false confidence but honest assessment.

Somatic Awareness: "What is my body telling me? Am I feeling anxiety about performance or excitement about growth?" Often, impostor syndrome manifests as physical tension that clouds our thinking.

Relational Intelligence: "How are others responding to my work? What feedback am I receiving versus what I'm imagining?"

Purpose Alignment: "Does this challenge align with my *Ikigai*, or am I pursuing something that doesn't fit my authentic path?"

Integration Capacity: "How can I use available resources, including AI tools, to support my confidence without becoming dependent on external validation?"

We can generally measure performance, such as how fast you can run or how high you can jump, but measuring our potential is much more challenging. Anupama Lal, who has spent her career in learning and development, told me this:

"In my reflections, many of us tend to underestimate our own potential and strengths, finding it difficult to fully recognize what we do well and just how well we do it. Some of us, in contrast, may over amplify our achievements. For most, striking the right balance, genuinely acknowledging and owning our abilities, remains an area of opportunity.

Another important question is whether we can truly embody our strengths. In truth, it takes a lot of effort to be both deeply confident in our abilities and entirely authentic about it.

Cultivating a genuine sense of confidence comes from intentional effort and a shift in mindset, not from quick fixes or superficial strategies. Perhaps most unexpectedly, confident humility is often grounded in something many leadership books overlook: self-love."

THE SURPRISE OF SELF-LOVE

"Talk to yourself like you would to someone you love"
— *Brené Brown*

I sat in the University of Nottingham auditorium, waiting to witness my eldest daughter graduate. The air was thick with parents' pride and students' excitement as they sat in their gowns and mortarboards, eager to be called and receive their degrees.

The dean spoke about the university's values: curiosity, critical thinking, and compassion. He articulated the students' potential to make a difference and then introduced an alumnus to give the graduation speech.

The speaker, Dr. Chidinma Raymond-Limejuice, a molecular virology researcher, shared her journey as a student. She shared the challenges of moving from Nigeria to the United Kingdom to do her Master's and then her doctorate, and then she said something that made my ears prick up:

"Self-love is the path to understanding your potential"

I contacted Dr. Chidinma to understand how she came to this insight.

"In the second semester of my Master's, I found myself doing a lot of self-talking, and I honestly don't know where I learned that, but it made a lot of difference. I found myself self-encouraging and self-advising, and I'd say, 'Chidinma, you have to do this.'"

Because she was now away from her supportive family, Chidinma used a self-leadership strategy for self-motivation. Her self-awareness was that she only did well in subjects she loved, so if she didn't like the topic or lecturer, she would edit the narrative to only say good things to herself.

Chidinma had a clear vision of why and when she would complete her doctorate (2022) and had made a vision board to keep herself focused.

"Self-love is the path to understanding potential because self-love is about knowing me and understanding me, and inside of me is my potential"

I love this quote, and it reinforces my experience coaching people to access their confidence and amplify their potential. Often, clients tell me that they lack confidence, but after some probing questions, the real problem reveals itself: a lack of self-love.

Self-love is valuing and caring for oneself through actions that support physical, psychological, and spiritual growth. Self-love is foundational to potentializing because it fuels agency, resilience, and authenticity.

If you find it difficult to accept and love yourself, try this perspective shift: think about something in your world that you accept without judgment. Maybe your garden doesn't always bloom perfectly, or your favorite coffee shop sometimes runs out of your preferred pastry. You don't take it personally. You adapt and move on.

Now here's the question: what would change if you extended that same patient acceptance to yourself? Not lowering your standards, but recognizing that being human means being imperfect, learning, and growing. That's not self-indulgence. That's sanity.

Dr. Chidinma's insight about self-love being the path to potential connects directly to the NURTURE element of growth. You can't sustainably potentialize from a place of self-criticism and doubt.

WHEN VULNERABILITY BECOMES STRENGTH

Sometimes the most significant test of confident humility comes not in moments of triumph, but when life strips away all pretense and forces you to face your own mortality.

In 2021, my doctor called with news that challenged everything I thought I knew about control: "Andrew, your blood test shows a cancer marker. You'll need a CT scan and a colonoscopy."

Until that moment, I hadn't considered that I might have cancer. Suddenly, without the CT scan, I both had cancer and didn't, a medical version of Schrödinger's cat.

This is where confident humility gets tested. Conventional wisdom says, "think positive," but confident humility requires something more nuanced: facing brutal reality while maintaining faith that you will prevail, regardless of the outcome.

The CT scan revealed a large, suspicious mass requiring major surgery. As someone who had spent decades teaching self-leadership, I suddenly faced the ultimate reminder: some things are beyond our control.

But here's what confident humility taught me: acknowledging what you cannot control strengthens your ability to lead what you can.

I couldn't control the mass, surgery, or outcome. But I could control my response, how I prepared my family, organized my affairs, and approached recovery. Most importantly, I could control how I used this experience to deepen my understanding of being authentically human.

After six hours of surgery and three days of post-operative fever, the surgeon brought the news my wife and I had hoped for: "The histology is benign; you don't have cancer."

The relief was overwhelming. But the real gift wasn't the clean pathology report; it was discovering that you can face your deepest fears with courage, humility, strength, and vulnerability.

Facing that potential diagnosis forced me to EVALU-ATE what truly mattered and TRANSFORM how I thought about control. I couldn't control the outcome, but I could control my response; that's confident humility in its rawest form.

As Dr. Chidinma said in her graduation speech, "Self-love is the path to understanding your potential." Sometimes that path leads through hospital corridors and forces you to love yourself not because you're strong, but because you are courageously human.

The paradox of confident humility: The more honestly we face our limitations, the more we discover our true strength. The more we accept our vulnerability, the more courageous we become. The more we acknowledge what we cannot control, the more effectively we can lead what we can.

This experience didn't make me more confident about avoiding future health challenges, it made me more confident in my ability to face whatever comes with strength and grace. That's the difference between arrogant certainty and confident humility: one pretends to have all the answers, the other trusts in the ability to find them as needed.

Confident humility requires one crucial skill that many leaders struggle with: knowing when to say no. This isn't just boundary-setting; it's an act of self-love that preserves energy for what matters most.

SAYING NO IS AN ACT OF SELF-LOVE

"To thine own self be true"
*– Polonius in **Hamlet** by William Shakespeare*

"No" is the boundary word. Saying "No" is a powerful expression of self-leadership and self-love. It affirms that you are responsible for your time, energy, and emotional well-being and that you are consciously choosing what aligns with your values, purpose, and potential. Every "Yes" is a commitment of time and attention. Saying "No" strategically is how self-leaders preserve bandwidth for what matters most.

If you don't establish boundaries, your goals become secondary to other people's agendas. A clear "No" signals that you are anchored in your values and priorities and not swayed by guilt, obligation, or fear of disapproval.

When you say "No" respectfully but firmly, you model self-respect, which often earns respect in return. People begin to take your time and energy seriously.

While people-pleasing may feel generous, it often leads to emotional depletion, misalignment, and eventual resentment. A healthy "No" is a long-term "Yes" to your well-being and contribution.

How to Say "No' Like a Self-Leader

1. Be clear and direct – don't over-explain. Clarity is kindness.

   "*Thanks for thinking of me. I can't commit to this right now.*"

2. Offer an alternative – if appropriate.

   "*I'm not available for that, but I can suggest someone who might be.*"

3. Hold your line with grace. You don't owe everyone an explanation. Silence after your "No" is allowed.

4. Say "No" so you can say "Yes" to what matters. Every "No" is a strategic "Yes" to something more aligned with your purpose and potential.

Surprisingly, when you say "No" as an act of self-love, you are more likely to be liked and respected. If people only like you because you say "Yes," is that a healthy relationship?

Setting boundaries by saying "No" builds one's foundation of confidence and humility. But another crucial element is developing the belief that you can handle whatever challenges come your way. This belief doesn't emerge from thin air. It grows through specific experiences that teach you a fundamental truth: you're more capable than you think.

Confident humility isn't just a nice-to-have personality trait. In the AI age, it becomes your survival skill – secure enough in your abilities to partner with AI, humble enough to keep learning when everything changes.

FINDING YOUR "I CAN DO THIS" MOMENT

"Accidents, try to change them – it's impossible. The accidental reveals man"

– J.B. Priestly

Let me tell you about Christine. She was part of a group climbing Mount Kilimanjaro with my friend Erik, an adventure leader. On the first evening, this teenager cornered Erik and declared, "I hate you. My mother forced me to do this. I want to go back."

Erik was puzzled. Christine had been the first to sign up, saying it was her father's dream to climb the mountain before he passed away 18 months earlier.

"Nobody forced you," Erik told her gently. "You signed up because you wanted to do this." Something shifted. The next day, Christine was first in line to climb. She became one of the strongest team members and was the first to reach the summit.

What changed? Christine found her "I can do this" moment.

Psychologist Albert Bandura calls this self-efficacy, the belief that you can handle whatever challenge you face. It's different from general confidence because it's situation-specific. For example, you might have high self-efficacy for public speaking, like me, but low self-efficacy for rock climbing, also like me.

Bandura discovered that self-efficacy is more predictive of success than actual skill level. The person who believes, "I can figure this out," will outperform the more skilled person who thinks, "I'm probably going to mess this up."

Dalia Feldheim, author of *Lead Like a Girl*, discovered confident humility on a gymnastics mat in Israel when she was just a child (Feldheim, 2024). She told me:

> *"As a competitive gymnast, my biggest lesson was competing against myself. It's always about being the best you can be and improving daily. I learned the importance of discipline, self-driven discipline."*

The real test came during a national competition where Dalia was expected to place first. She performed brilliantly until the final apparatus.

"I got stuck in the rope and lost half a point. I came in second instead of first."

Her coach's immediate reaction was frustration: "How did you get stuck? You never get stuck! How did we lose this competition?"

But Dalia's mother stepped between them with a reframe that would shape her daughter's relationship with achievement forever: "What are you talking about? It's her first competition and she's already number two. We're going out to celebrate."

That moment taught Dalia something profound about potential: it's not about being perfect or always winning. It's about competing against your previous best self while maintaining perspective about the journey.

"I never got to number one. I was number two, then number three. But then something else kicked in, coaching others. Because I was the eldest, I became a little mother to the younger gymnasts."

When her protégés began surpassing her rankings, Dalia's potential proprioception helped her make a decision, demonstrating wisdom far beyond her 13 years.

"When they overtook me to become number three, two, and one, I was so proud of them. I realized I don't need to be number one because I want to enjoy the ride."

Rather than becoming bitter or quitting, she transformed her identity from competitor to developer of others. At 14, she became one of the youngest national coaches in Israel, bringing her gymnasts to competitions.

"I learned two things that shaped everything afterward: the importance of hard work and internal motivation, and I learned the value of giving back."

This early experience created the foundation for self-efficacy and confident humility, serving Dalia throughout her corporate career. She learned to maintain high personal standards without needing external validation, celebrate others' success without diminishing her worth, and find new ways to contribute when circumstances change.

When you can separate your self-worth from your performance ranking, maintain high standards while celebrating others' success, and transform setbacks into new opportunities to contribute, that's confident humility in action. The sweet spot between arrogance and self-doubt allows potential to flourish sustainably over decades.

THE FOUR PILLARS OF SELF-EFFICACY

Bandura identified four ways to build lasting self-efficacy.

1. **Progressive Mastery:** Don't bite off more than you can chew. Increase challenges gradually so each success builds on the previous one. Christine didn't start by summiting Kilimanjaro; she started by showing up on day two.

2. **Vicarious Experience:** Watch others succeed at what you want to do. This is why biographies matter, why mentors matter, why seeing someone "like you" achieve something expands your sense of possibility.

3. **Social Persuasion:** Having people who believe in you matters. But here's the catch: cheerleading alone doesn't work. It needs to be combined with actual opportunities to succeed.

4. **Emotional Regulation:** Learn to reframe your physiological responses. Those butterflies before a big presentation? That's not fear, that's your body getting ready to perform.

As an exercise, try mapping the four pillars of self-efficacy onto the Potential Proprioception framework.

THE MOST POWERFUL MOMENT

Talent strategist, Steve Cadigan, told me: "If you ask any executive what the most impactful moment was in their career arc, I guarantee you they're gonna tell you, I had this boss, they put me in this job I didn't think I was ready for, I didn't think I was qualified for, and I was scared, and it was the greatest experience of my life. Tackling something new. I didn't have experience. I didn't think I was prepared. I'm thinking, 'I'm not ready for that. I need more experience.' And it just blew their mind and completely raised their confidence level of what's possible."

Steve highlighted that in Silicon Valley, where the most valuable companies in the world are located, most people are doing something they've never done before in their lives, and at scale.

"And look what's happening. . ." he said. "When you put someone in a position of doing something they've never done before, you are unlocking magic. You're unlocking energy."

THE COMFORT ZONE MYTH

"Comfort is a drug. Once you get used to it, it's hard to give up"
– Henry Cavill

"Get out of your comfort zone!" We hear this everywhere, from motivational speakers to social media memes. But they don't tell you that comfort zones serve a purpose.

Your body has comfort zones for temperature, blood sugar, and oxygen levels. Step too far outside these zones, and you die. Your mind has comfort zones, too, which keep you from taking genuinely dangerous risks.

The advice is not wrong; it's incomplete. The key is expanding your comfort zone through progressive challenges, not making radical leaps that set you up for failure.

Think of it like physical training. You don't go from the couch to a marathon in one day. You build gradually, letting your body adapt to increased demands. Your confidence works the same way.

Here's the truth most people miss: we don't know the limits of our potential. But we can expand those limits systematically, like a snowball rolling downhill and gathering momentum.

In coaching practice, I've found that when people attempt to step out of their comfort zone by making one or more huge changes, they set themselves up for failure. Instead, clarify which aspect of potential you wish to maximize, set an intention to do so, and follow through, starting with small actions and gradually increasing the challenge. By doing this, you follow a proven psychological path to growing your locus of control and developing skills and capabilities.

Performance influences self-efficacy beliefs, which influence future performance. This creates a self-reinforcing loop. See Figure 5.2.

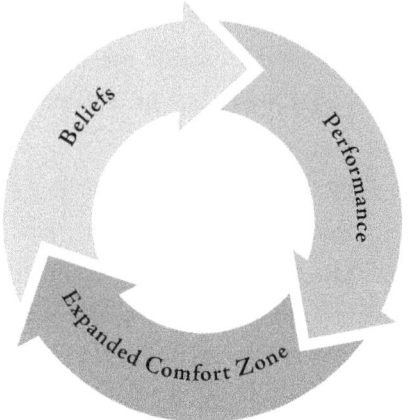

Figure 5.2   The Comfort Zone

THERE IS NO PERFORMANCE WITHOUT PRACTICE

Zig Ziglar, the American author, salesman, and motivational speaker, famously said: "Success occurs when opportunity meets preparation."

There is no better preparation than practice; maximizing potential requires intentional practice, which involves intentionally influencing thinking, feelings, and actions toward objectives, also known as self-leadership.

Sportspeople and military personnel understand that 95% of their time is spent on development and only 5% on competing or combat.

In the corporate world, it is the other way around. Depending on the organization, people may get much less than 5% of their time designated for development.

The "10,000-Hour Rule" is a concept popularized by Malcolm Gladwell in his 2008 book *Outliers* (Gladwell, 2008). It suggests that achieving expertise in any skill requires approximately 10,000 hours of deliberate practice.

The rule originates from research by psychologist Anders Ericsson and colleagues, who studied elite violinists at Berlin's Academy of Music in the early 1990s. They found that the most accomplished musicians had accumulated about 10,000 hours of practice by age 20, significantly more than less accomplished performers.

Gladwell's "magic number of greatness" has been widely criticized. Subsequent research shows that mastery requires deliberate practice quality rather than just accumulated hours, and that the time required to achieve expertise varies greatly across domains.

Here's what really creates expertise: yes, you need practice, but intentional practice beats mindless repetition every time. You need some natural ability (sorry, not everyone can be Mozart). You need decent teachers and the right opportunities. Most importantly, you need to actually care about getting better.

Try This: Cultivate Confident Humility

Confident humility becomes essential for each element of AI collaboration.

You can't INSPIRE an AI system or human team if you're operating from arrogant certainty or paralyzing self-doubt. You need the balance that says, "I have valuable insights to contribute" while remaining "curious about what I might be missing."[2]

To effectively INTEGRATE with AI tools, you need enough confidence to direct them strategically and enough humility to learn from what they reveal. . .

INSPIRE: Write your "I can do this" statement for a current challenge, but add: "... and I'm curious to learn what I don't know yet."

GUIDE: Identify one person who demonstrates confident humility. Observe how they handle uncertainty and mistakes.

NURTURE: Practice the self-love acceptance exercise, then extend that same compassion to your learning process.

INTEGRATE: Use AI tools to get feedback on your blind spots, but make your own decision about how to act on that information.

TRANSFORM: Take on one challenge that requires you to be confident about your abilities while humble about your knowledge.

EVALUATE: Ask each evening, "Did I operate from confident humility today, or did I slide toward arrogance or self-doubt?"

Confident humility opens the door to our most distinct human superpowers: curiosity and creativity. These are the forces that transform potential into innovation and routine into breakthroughs.

When you operate from confident humility, you create the perfect conditions for wonder to emerge. You're secure enough in your abilities to ask questions that might expose what you don't know. You're humble enough to be genuinely surprised by what you discover. This combination becomes the launching pad for the two capabilities no algorithm can replicate: insatiable curiosity about the world around you and the creative capacity to imagine what doesn't yet exist.

The leaders who will thrive alongside AI aren't those who know the most, but those who remain most curious about what they don't know and most creative about what could be possible.

CHAPTER 6

THE WONDER DRUG: WHY CURIOSITY IS YOUR CREATIVITY STEROID

"The important thing is not to stop questioning. Curiosity has its own reason for existing"

– Albert Einstein,

"Old man's advice to youth: Never lose a holy curiosity"

Confident humility creates the perfect conditions for wonder to emerge. When you're secure enough in your abilities to ask questions that might expose what you don't know, and humble enough to be genuinely surprised by what you discover, you unlock humanity's most distinctive advantage: insatiable curiosity.

But here's what most people miss about curiosity: it's not just about being interested in things. It's your creativity steroid, the catalyst that transforms routine thinking into breakthrough innovation. While AI can process information at superhuman speeds, it cannot experience the existential wonder that drives human discovery. That wonder, that need to poke at things we don't understand, might be the thing that makes us irreplaceably human.

Consider this: every breakthrough in human history started with someone being curious about something that everyone else took for granted. Today, as AI handles more of our routine cognitive work, curiosity becomes our competitive edge, not just for individuals, but for our species.

I interviewed Dr. Diane Hamilton as she was writing *Cracking the Curiosity Code: The Key to Unlocking Human Potential* (Hamilton, 2019).

Hamilton spent years researching what every toddler's parent learns within approximately 48 hours: curious people are exhausting, persistent, and absolutely unstoppable. The difference is that Hamilton figured out how to weaponize this insight for good instead of hiding in the bathroom with a cup of coffee.

During the interview, Diane and I discussed why curiosity dramatically decreases as we age.

This decline isn't due to a natural loss of curiosity but to various inhibiting factors we have identified as dragons to be reframed and ridden.

- **Fear:** Concern about looking unprepared or incompetent.
- **Assumptions:** Self-limiting beliefs about what will or won't interest us.

- **Technology:** Either over-reliance or resistance to technological change.
- **Environment:** Influence of family, education, workplace, and social contexts.

In Frank Herbert's *Dune*, the young Prince Atreides is told:

> *"Fear is the mind-killer. Fear is the little death that brings obliteration. I will face my fear and I will permit it to pass over me and through me"*

By identifying your fear, you can learn to face it.

Most of us were raised on a steady diet of "don't talk to strangers" and "because I said so." Perfectly sensible for keeping five-year-olds alive, but terrible preparation for navigating a world where the strange and different often hold the keys to breakthrough thinking.

We must rewire ourselves from cautious consumers of approved knowledge into curious anthropologists of possibility.

Psychology professor Todd Kashdan has spent years studying what kills curiosity in the workplace. He found that it's not that people aren't naturally curious, it's that most organizations accidentally crush that curiosity without realizing it.

"Give people even the smallest choice in what they explore," Kashdan explains, "and watch what happens."

The research backs this up beautifully (Schutte, 2019).
When employees can choose which problem to tackle
rather than having it assigned, their engagement doesn't just
improve, it skyrockets.

Think about it: when was the last time you felt genuinely excited about a task someone else picked for you versus
something you chose to dive into? That's autonomy working its magic on curiosity. It doesn't take much, just enough
choice to make people feel they have some say in their own
learning journey.

Curiosity is integral to self-learning, but how can we
boost curiosity?

The Hole in the Wall

In 1999, Dr. Sugata Mitra was curious about how children
might interact with computers without formal instruction.

He decided to experiment in a slum in New Delhi, India
(Mitra, 2005). Mitra's team cut a hole in the boundary wall
separating his office from the adjacent slum and installed a
computer with a touchpad connected to the internet. The
computer was placed at a height accessible to children, with
the screen and touchpad facing the slum area. No instructions were provided, and no announcement was made about
the installation.

The computer was left there, with a hidden camera
recording the interactions.

Within hours, curious children from the slum, most of
whom had never seen a computer before and did not know

English (the operating system language), began to explore the device. The researchers observed remarkable patterns:

1. Children first approached individually, but quickly formed collaborative groups.
2. A child who discovered something new would teach others.
3. Younger children often watched from the periphery and then participated after observing.
4. Within days, children had taught themselves basic computer operations like clicking, dragging, and browsing.
5. Within weeks, they had discovered how to draw, play games, and browse the internet.
6. Children developed their own vocabulary to describe computer functions.

The most striking finding was that no adult intervention was required. The children's natural curiosity and collaborative problem-solving led to substantial learning.

After the initial experiment's success, Mitra expanded the project to other locations across India. In one notable case, in the village of Kalikuppam, children with no prior knowledge of English or science education taught themselves biotechnology concepts in English by using the computer and working together. When tested, they scored nearly as well as students from a privileged Delhi school.

This experiment formed the foundation for Mitra's development of self-organized learning environments (SOLEs) and his broader educational philosophy that emphasizes minimally invasive education and children's innate capacity for self-directed learning, regardless of the environment.

José Urbina López Primary School sits next to a dump just across the US border in Mexico. The school serves residents of Matamoros, a dusty, sunbaked city of 489,000 that is a flash point in the war on drugs. There are regular shoot-outs, and it's not uncommon for locals to find bodies scattered in the street in the morning. To get to the school, students walk along a white dirt road that parallels a fetid canal (Davis, 2019).

By conventional metrics, this should be where potential goes to die.

Inspired by Dr. Sugata Mitra's approach, teacher Sergio Juárez Correa implemented a creative teaching method.

One of Sergio's students, Paloma Noyola Bueno, the daughter of a junkyard worker, went from struggling to being ranked as one of the top math students in Mexico. In 2012, Sergio's class scored in the 99.99th percentile in mathematics on the national exam.

Had Sergio Juárez Correa drilled through the desert to find the reservoir of creative potential beneath, or had it bubbled up under pressure?

Boost Your Curiosity

> "Everybody has potential; the secret is to help them understand what that means for them and feel like they can be a better version of themselves"
>
> — Shane Kidwell, Headmaster

You can train your curiosity by making tasks personally relevant. Remind yourself or others about the usefulness of new knowledge and how it connects with goals or objectives. If you find your curiosity lagging, compile a list of questions that you would like to find answers to. Studies (Shelby Clark, 2019) have found that using this simple step to identify the current gaps in your knowledge naturally sparks more curiosity. For example:

- What questions are you not asking because you assume you already know the answers?
- If you could only ask questions for a week without making any statements, what would you discover?
- What topic do you avoid exploring because you fear what you might learn?
- How might your expertise in one area create blind spots in others?
- If you approached your biggest challenge with the curiosity of a five-year-old, what would you notice differently?

Dr. Hamilton's podcast interviews with successful individuals, including billionaires like Keith Krach, former CEO of DocuSign, consistently reveal that maintaining curiosity is crucial for success. She notes that successful individuals share a common trait of being "endlessly curious" and constantly seeking to learn about new industries and ideas.

In today's rapidly changing world, curiosity becomes even more crucial:

- AI and technological advancement require continuous learning
- Complex problems need creative solutions
- Competitive advantages come from innovation and adaptation
- Career success depends on the ability to learn and evolve

DIVERSIFY YOUR EXPERIENCES

Another way to boost your curiosity is through "Ligrothism," which is the art of diversifying one's life experience and expanding one's comfort zone to have better stories to tell. Ligrothism is formed by combining the words "live" and "grow" and adding "ism," the suffix meaning philosophy.

Columbia business professor and *Wall Street Journal* best-selling author Dorie Clark credits her mother with encouraging her confidence, curiosity, and the desire to expand her comfort zone.

"I'm very grateful to my mom, who was very encouraging. She did things that were annoying to me at the time. Her philosophy was, I want you to be exposed to everything so you can see what you love and what you're good at."

"Part of that involved her forcing me to take ballet, tap, and piano lessons. Needless to say, none of these made my heart sing. And I'm just like, Oh God, please. But, uh, but you know, that was the price to pay because she also let me do the things I was interested in."

"And so, I played sports and did guitar, and she sent me to summer programs and arranged a G.I. Joe scavenger hunt for my seventh birthday. I appreciated these opportunities. It's marvelous if we get this chance as children, but as adults, we can do this for ourselves."

Dorie's mother understood that diversified experiences and imagination are key to realizing potential, so we must encourage these as early as possible.

It is therefore concerning that today's youth are not typically reading books. They're stuck on devices, watching videos and short clips on TikTok.

When you read, you must engage your imagination to picture what you are reading, but when you watch a movie, you don't have to do that; the director has already done it for you.

My friend and colleague, Fredrik Haren, an expert on creativity, lives on a beautiful island in Stockholm as a direct result of his curiosity-driven thinking.

Most people, when looking for a place to live, ask the conventional question: "Should I buy an apartment in the north or south of the city?"

Instead of accepting those limited options, Fredrik let his curiosity run wild: "I said, you know what, let's go crazy. How could I possibly live? And I thought it would be cool to have my own island."

Most people would dismiss this as fantasy. Fredrik turned it into research: "I said, okay, let's see if there's any island for sale. And it turned out that I could buy an island for the same price I could buy an apartment for."

Today, Fredrik lives on a beautiful private island 15 minutes from central Stockholm.

The power wasn't in the answer but in asking the right question.

"Just by broadening my perspective on the potential of how I live my life, where I sleep and spend my days, I would say, a million times better than if I hadn't done that."

But Fredrik's curiosity didn't stop there. He practices what he calls "island upgrades," constantly asking, "How can I make this even better?" This led to adding a sauna, which then sparked another curious question: "What are we going to do with it when we're not using the sauna?" The answer: a home cinema with a removable projector.

The lesson: Curiosity isn't just about wondering how things work, it's about questioning the assumptions that limit your options. When everyone else was asking, "North side or south side of the city?" Fredrik was asking, "What if I don't have to choose either?"

As Fredrik puts it, "Creativity gives you options, creativity gives you alternatives, creativity is unimagined potential."

The next time you face a decision, don't just accept the obvious options. Ask Fredrik's question: "What could possibly be?" Your answer might be living on an island, or something even better that you haven't imagined yet.

THE ALCHEMY OF CURIOSITY: WHY AI CAN'T WONDER

History has been unkind to alchemists, dismissing them as dungeon-dwelling weirdos obsessed with turning lead into gold. But that's like calling Steve Jobs a guy who was really into calligraphy. The alchemists weren't failed scientists, they were the original interdisciplinary thinkers, the first people crazy enough to believe that understanding and transforming reality through persistent investigation was actually possible.

Without them, we would not have chemistry, the scientific method, cross-cultural knowledge transfer, and, most importantly, the belief that humans could understand and transform reality through persistent investigation.

AI can process information, but cannot experience the existential wonder that drives human curiosity. Human curiosity emerges from our mortality, dreams, and embodied limitations, things AI will never possess.

AI Versus Human Approach to Alchemy

AI Processing	Human Curiosity
Analyzes historical texts efficiently	Wonders: "What if transformation is possible?"
Sorts ideas into categories	Seeks unified understanding across domains
Can identify errors in methods	Appreciates the beauty of the attempt
Optimizes outcomes based on data	Driven by hope and existential questions

Curiosity opens doors, but creativity walks through them. While curiosity asks "What if?" creativity answers "Why not?" Together, they form the foundation of human potential that no algorithm can replicate.

CREATIVITY

I mentioned my friend Fredrik Haren, who lives on an island in Stockholm. His home office is a transparent geodesic dome with stunning 360-degree panoramic views. The perfect environment to write and conduct interviews with creative people around the world.

Typically, when I talk to people about potential, they default to thinking about it in terms of performance. However, performance is contextual, while potential is much like Fredrik's geodesic dome; it is multifaceted and 360-degree.

Potential is not unimaginable; it's just that many people have not yet imagined what is possible for them. They have been stuck with a mindset, but with creativity, they can imagine alternative scenarios and see what else they could do with their life and careers.

Sometimes, circumstances or geography block our view of potential. There are many stories of people who have moved countries, and suddenly, a whole new world of possibilities opens up.

Fredrik has spent 25 years traveling to more than 75 countries, interviewing thousands of creative individuals from choreographers in Copenhagen to nomads in Mongolia, from children in Mumbai's slums to government officials in Bhutan. The result is a kaleidoscopic view of creativity that challenges assumptions about innovation, originality, and the creative process itself.

Global learning and development expert Artem Ivanenko uses the video game *Civilization* as an analogy.

With each turn, players build their cities and explore more of the map to discover resources.

Travel broadens the mind and shows us new options and opportunities. We can also use the power of our imagination to explore potential possibilities.

Alan Bennet, the English actor, author, and playwright, said:

"A book is a device to ignite the imagination"

This was true for me when I was young and was transported to different realities through reading.

Fredrik told me, "I feel sad for the creative people who are not doing enough to develop their creative potential fully. I don't feel sad for the short basketball player; I feel sad for the tall basketball player who doesn't practice every day to become the best basketball player they can be."

Fredrik believes that creativity is the human superpower when it comes to potential. You see it in children; ask a preschool child to imagine something impossible, and they will do just that. Ask an adult to do the same, and they will regurgitate something they have already heard. Fredrik says, "We enter school as poets and come out parrots!"

Curiosity and creativity unlock your potential, but if you want to maximize performance and inspire excellence, you also need to be doing things.

I spoke with Wanda Naomi Rau, a former leader at The Walt Disney Company, about the creative partnership between humans and AI.

Wanda believes AI can amplify what makes us extraordinary, but it will never replace us. She shared a quote with me:

"As technology becomes capable of creating soulless perfection, so we hunger for imperfection, for the rough beauty that bears the imprint of the fallible human hand"
— Dinah Hall

This quote reminded me of Kintsugi, the Japanese practice of repairing broken pottery with gold. Instead of hiding flaws, it turns them into features.

As AI grows more "perfect," our edge isn't in competing with it but in embracing what makes us irreplaceably human.

As humans, we can see the story in broken and repaired pottery. Stories tell us who we are; they capture the pain and triumph of our human journey.

COMPARISON KILLS POTENTIAL

"Comparison is the seat of all unhappiness"
— The Buddha

We have previously discussed "impostor syndrome," which results from unfavorable comparisons with others. Many people feel that they are not creative or don't have potential because they compare themselves with people who excel in a particular field. If you have a friend or sibling who excels at music or math, but you struggle with these, you might conclude that you are not creative.

While comparison can lead to unhappiness, self-assessment – such as the Potential Proprioception framework – can help us assess which areas of our lives and careers need to be creatively developed.

You Are on an Adventure

To be creative is to be an adventurer. An adventure is any undertaking whose outcome is uncertain, which perfectly describes partnering with AI in today's rapidly changing world.

Think about it: every interaction with AI is fundamentally uncertain. You don't know what insights it might reveal, what connections it might suggest, or what possibilities it might uncover. The leaders who thrive alongside AI don't fear this uncertainty, they embrace it with the curiosity of explorers.

The entrepreneurial mindset becomes essential here. Do you know the origin of the word entrepreneur? It comes from the French *entrependre*, meaning to undertake, specifically, to undertake a journey into unknown territory. Today's most successful AI collaborators approach each project with this same spirit: curious about what they might discover, prepared for unexpected challenges, excited by uncertain outcomes.

Entrepreneurship represents one of the most demanding paths of personal and professional development.

Silicon Valley investors often prefer founders who have experienced failure, embodying the maxim to "fail forward."

When approached with the right mindset, failure represents a setback and an opportunity for profound learning and growth.

Every adventure has a defining moment, the point where you're pushed beyond what you thought you could handle. For entrepreneurs, it's often called "the valley of death." For adventurers, it might be the storm that tests everything you've learned.

In your journey to unlock potential, this moment isn't optional, it's essential. Curiosity and creativity prepare you for the adventure, but it's how you respond when that adventure gets difficult that determines whether potential becomes performance. That crucible of adversity isn't something to avoid. It's the catalyst that transforms possibility into power.

TRY THIS: REIGNITE CURIOSITY, REWIRE CREATIVITY

Curiosity is the gateway to creativity; creativity is how we access our potential in nonlinear, transformative ways. Use the Potential Proprioception framework to help you break habitual thinking patterns and see from new angles.

SELF-LEADERSHIP AWARENESS CHECK

Rate yourself honestly (1–5 scale) on the following.

- **Questioning Habit:** How often do you ask "What if?" or "Why not?" instead of accepting things as they are?

- **Learning Stance:** Are you approaching challenges as solving problems or exploring mysteries?
- **Fear Awareness:** What assumptions are you not questioning because you're afraid of looking foolish?

Proprioceptive insight: If you scored below 3 on any item, your curiosity muscles have atrophied from disuse.

COMPETENCE INTELLIGENCE ASSESSMENT

Map your current learning edge.

- **Known Territory:** What do you feel genuinely confident about?
- **Learning Zone:** What are you actively curious about right now?
- **Mystery Territory:** What intimidates you but also intrigues you?

Creative action: Pick one item from your Mystery Territory and spend 10 minutes researching it this week. Notice how your intimidation shifts to fascination.

SOMATIC AWARENESS STRETCH

Explore how improvisational theatre works and see how leaders can foster innovation by creating "yes, and" cultures instead of shutting ideas down too early.

RELATIONAL INTELLIGENCE EXPANSION

Curiosity thrives in connection.

- **Curiosity Partners:** Who in your network asks the best questions?
- **Learning Communities:** Where do you go to explore ideas without judgment?
- **Perspective Gaps:** What viewpoints are missing from your usual conversations?

Try this week: Have one conversation with someone whose expertise or perspective is completely different from yours. Ask them: "What's the most interesting problem you're working on right now?"

INTEGRATION CAPACITY EXPERIMENT (ONGOING)
Use AI as your curiosity amplifier, not replacement.

- **Question Generation:** Ask AI to help you generate better questions about topics you're exploring.
- **Connection Mapping:** Use AI to find unexpected connections between your interests.
- **Learning Acceleration:** Let AI handle research grunt work so you can focus on synthesis and application.

Boundary: Never let AI's answers stop your questioning. Use its responses as jumping-off points for deeper exploration.

Curiosity and creativity unlock your potential by expanding what you believe is possible. They help you see opportunities where others see obstacles, and imagine solutions that don't yet exist. But potential without testing remains theoretical. Creativity without challenges stays comfortable.

The bridge between having potential and realizing it isn't found in more brainstorming sessions or creativity workshops. It's forged in the crucible of adversity, where your curiosity gets tested under pressure and your creativity must deliver real solutions to real problems.

Every person who has truly unlocked their potential has a story about the moment when life demanded more than they thought they could give. That's where we turn our attention next: to the catalyst that transforms possibility into performance.

CHAPTER 7

ADVERSITY – THE CATALYST THAT TRANSFORMS POTENTIAL INTO PERFORMANCE

"The most beautiful people we have known are those who have known defeat, known suffering, known struggle, known loss, and have found their way out of the depths"

– Elisabeth Kübler-Ross

Curiosity and creativity prepare you for the adventure, but it's how you respond when that adventure gets difficult that determines whether potential becomes performance. Every breakthrough story has a moment when circumstances demand more than the person thought they could give. That's where Aaron Phipps, MBE, found himself at 15.

Aaron was not supposed to become a Paralympic champion or the first person to scale Kilimanjaro on their hands and knees. He was a B-grade student who had discovered alcohol and wasn't going anywhere. His life was what he calls "magnolia," the bland, off-white paint color that dominated British homes. Unremarkable. Forgettable. Safe.

Then meningitis and sepsis took his legs and most of his fingers. Two weeks in a coma. A year in the hospital. Most people would call this the end of potential. Aaron called it the beginning.

"I remember quite quickly, saying to my mum that I was going to beat this." It wasn't defiance or denial; it was something more profound. In that hospital bed, facing a reality no teenager should face, Aaron discovered the catalytic quality of adversity: it doesn't reveal who you are, it reveals who you can become.

You might think this chapter is going to be "emotionally heavy," but it isn't about going through pain or becoming disabled to unlock potential; it's about understanding how adversity, whether chosen or imposed, physical or financial, can become the catalyst for us to potentialize and to inspire others to excellence.

And let's be real: nobody is going to be inspired by a story about someone whose success just fell into their lap.

The Failure Premium Phenomenon

Aaron's story illustrates something Silicon Valley has known for years: adversity isn't the enemy of potential, it's the catalyst that reveals it. Job candidates or founders seeking funding are perceived as having more potential if they have previously failed but learned from that failure.

Today's roles require dealing with uncertainty, and building a company is 90% dealing with things going wrong, so you want to know how someone handles adversity before you give them a job or $10 million.

As venture capitalist Josh Kopelman of First Round Capital puts it: "I'd rather back a founder who's failed once than one who's never been tested. The first-time founder might be brilliant, but the battle-tested founder knows how to survive when everything goes wrong."

An example of this would be LinkedIn's co-founder, Reid Hoffman, who started SocialNet.com in 1997. This was an early social networking site used for online dating and matching up people with similar interests, like golfers looking for neighborhood partners. The site failed to gain traction, but Hoffman learned about user adoption patterns and network effects. When he founded LinkedIn in 2002, Sequoia Capital knew that Hoffman understood what didn't work in social networking. When Microsoft acquired LinkedIn in 2016 for $26.2 billion, Hoffman received $2.8 billion, so not a bad payday for a "failure."

How Adversity Can IGNITE Potential

The IGNITE framework applies whether adversity chooses you or you choose it.

Inspire: Lying in a hospital bed, Aaron said, "Mum, I'm going to beat this." That was the spark, the spark of inspiration, on Aaron's journey to excellence as a wheelchair rugby gold-medal Paralympian.

Guide: The road to gold was not smooth. During his hospital stay, his determination demanded double physiotherapy to guide his recovery.

However, on returning home, life returned to being magnolia, and he again sought distraction by partying hard. "I think I was in my early twenties, having a midlife crisis. Because I was so aware of my mortality, all my friends were floating through life without a care in the world. But when you've stared death in the eye, you're wired differently.

I knew that I had to do something. I didn't know what my potential was, but a seed had been planted, I needed to do something, but I didn't know what that was."

He needed different guidance, and that came in the form of coaches.

Nurture: "I just started to take opportunities. I started to do wheelchair racing. I wanted to raise some money for charity, so I entered the local 10k race, did it in an everyday wheelchair, and loved it. Maybe in some ways, I was just looking for an out. I knew I couldn't do a mundane admin job for the rest of my life.

The wheelchair racing led me into the London Marathons, which led me into wheelchair rugby. From there, it was just me taking opportunities. It was just saying yes to things. And then, it's like you agree to something, then you work out how you're going to do it.

If you don't agree to anything in the first place, then nothing's going to happen."

Aaron's belief (self-efficacy) was being built through progressive challenges, and then he found a belonging in Paralympic sport.

From wheelchair marathons, Aaron transitioned to wheelchair rugby and played for Great Britain in the 2009 London Paralympics. The team didn't win a medal, but Aaron, as a new player, scored half of the team's points.

Integrate: Aaron needed to integrate technologies such as prosthetics and custom wheelchairs to compete in the Paralympics. He was self-trained in wheelchair marathons but had to integrate new training methods and team dynamics to be Paralympic-ready.

Transform: The road to the Paralympics had been challenging from a family, financial, and training perspective, so Aaron took a break from the sport. Then, in 2016, Aaron said "Yes" to another opportunity.

"Over the years, I've raised a quarter of a million pounds for the Meningitis Research Foundation, and they approached me to climb Mount Kilimanjaro to raise funds.

Other people have summited in wheelchairs, but they've been carried to the top. I wanted to do it by myself, so we set this goal to become the first person in the world to get to the top of Kilimanjaro in a wheelchair without any assistance.

Although I've got prosthetic legs as an amputee, I've got bad scars, so if I walk too much, my legs get sore. Day one was meant to take three hours; it took six.

Day two was meant to take four and a half hours; it took ten. Then they said, 'We're going to have to carry you.' I said, 'That's not happening.' When we talk about determination, this is probably the most determined I've ever been, apart from the gold-medal match in Tokyo.

I was like, there is no way I am going to be carried. I've told everybody that I'm going to do this. I had a set of knee pads with me, so I duct taped the knee pads to my legs, jumped out of my chair, and started crawling. But it was hard. It was really hard.

I was falling to bits. I was covered in blood, but there was no way I was going to get carried up that mountain."

I asked Aaron what he learned from this extreme experience. He told me that he had learned how far he could push himself, about preparation, and expanding his comfort zone. He had the self-efficacy to overcome the obstacles and achieve his objectives and full autonomy.

Through each progressive challenge, Aaron transformed from a "victim" to a "champion." His identity and story aligned with "I'm unstoppable."

Evaluate: Aaron returned to rugby and trained, through the pandemic, for the 2020 Tokyo Paralympics, where he and the team won gold for Great Britain.

Aaron now shares his journey through motivational speeches to create a spark for others. I asked him what advice he would give on finding meaning and achieving potential.

"You know, don't just bob along. That's boring. Don't be magnolia. But work. Don't just be content where you are. Go and ask your manager for some more responsibility. You only get one go on the merry go round, so push yourself. I think that's the, that's my message that I try and get to people. I had to lose 30% of my body before I started to use 100% of my potential!"

You Don't Need to Lose 30% of Your Body to Access 100% of Your Potential

Had Aaron Phipps, MBE, not found his mental toughness, he would not have summited Kilimanjaro and won Paralympic gold.

When looking for the potential in others, observe how they respond in unfamiliar and challenging situations. Do they exhibit self-belief and roll up their sleeves to work it out?

Personal resilience is essential, but potential truly flourishes in community. Aaron's journey from hospital bed to Paralympic gold required not just individual determination, but coaches who believed in him, teammates who supported him, and systems designed to develop rather than just evaluate talent.

What Adversity Teaches, But Success Does Not

Potential without pressure remains forever potential. It's adversity that transforms possibility into performance.

When everything goes well, you don't learn how to triage, prioritize, or maintain clarity when systems fail. Comfort zones don't require breakthrough thinking, but adversity does.

Abundant resources often lead to wasteful solutions; only time and money constraints force creative breakthroughs. Winning reinforces current assumptions and strategies rather than questioning and expanding perspective.

Easy times don't build the emotional muscle memory needed for genuine crises, and they reinforce the illusion of self-sufficiency. Only adversity reveals genuine relationships and our interdependence.

Adversity is not the enemy of potential; it's the catalyst that transforms potential into realized capability. Success validates what you already know; adversity teaches you what you didn't know you needed to learn.

This creates a paradox for new leaders and entrepreneurs:

- To get funding, you need experience.
- To get experience, you often need to fail.
- To fail, you first need to get funding.

With this in mind, many successful entrepreneurs now adopt a "failing fast and cheap" strategy, starting with minimal investment to gain the experience that venture capitalists value without the devastating personal cost.

WHAT DOESN'T KILL YOU...

Founder Melissa Goldner put it perfectly when she told me, "I'm not a survivor. I'm a surthriver." The difference? Survivors endure. Surthrivers grow stronger because of what they've been through.

That distinction matters because adversity is not the enemy.

Melissa's word, "surthriving," is what psychologists call post-traumatic growth. This is the positive psychological change that some individuals experience after a life crisis or traumatic event. Post-traumatic growth doesn't deny deep distress but instead suggests that adversity can unintentionally yield changes in understanding oneself, others, and the world.

"What doesn't kill you makes you stronger"

Nietzsche's famous quote comes from his 1888 work *Twilight of the Idols.*

The enduring popularity of this quote suggests it resonates with a fundamental human understanding that overcoming difficulties often leads to greater resilience and personal development. However, it's worth noting that Nietzsche's philosophy was more nuanced than this single phrase might suggest, and modern psychology recognizes that while adversity can lead to growth, it can also cause lasting harm if too severe or without proper support.

Don't Waste a Good Crisis

Kevin Gaskell didn't choose to inherit Porsche UK's disaster. The company was hemorrhaging money, customers hated them, and dealers had three years of unsold inventory gathering dust. When the Porsche family fired the entire board and called Kevin in, he faced what every leader dreads: adversity that was completely imposed on him.

Kevin could have played it safe, given them conventional answers, and probably kept his middle-management role. Instead, he chose to embrace the imposed adversity as an opportunity. "We will probably get fired," he told his colleague Armin, "we might as well tell them what we think."

That moment of accepting imposed adversity, rather than resisting or minimizing it, transformed Kevin from an operations manager to CEO at 32. The crisis he didn't create became the catalyst that revealed his leadership potential.

Kevin went on to turn the business around, and five years later, BMW hired him to head up its business in the UK.

Anneliese Olson volunteered for the unknown. When HP offered her an expat assignment to lead computing business in Asia, she could have stayed in her comfortable US role. Instead, she chose adversity.

"I was unknown; I didn't know anyone, so I was establishing myself," she told me. "My things were still on a boat from the USA to Singapore when we had a massive challenge in our China business.

The government was conducting consumer testing and evaluation, and we, like our competitors, used third-party power cords. However, we got some bad ratings, which resulted in the loss of hundreds of millions of dollars during this time.

This was a moment for rolling up my sleeves; this was in my accountability scope, what I was responsible for, but I was still learning the business, meeting the people, you know, figuring things out.

I had to travel from Singapore to China every four weeks and felt like a fish out of water. I didn't speak the language, but there was no one else.

I could ask people questions, which I did, my boss and others, but I had to figure it out myself and make the decisions. I asked, 'How do we go about doing this?' 'What structure can we provide?' 'What don't I know?' 'How do I lean on others?'

I used all my management, one-on-one, and business skills, aligning with groups of people quickly about the goals, what we needed to do, and how to create a recovery plan.

I did not want to waste a good crisis; I couldn't ignore it and needed to become an explorer.

Then, having spent two years in the China business, I became an expert in it because we were figuring it out. And to this day, the amount of credibility I have because of those behaviors and what I learned, helped me in my career because I could solve challenging problems."

Anneliese Olson now leads 9,000 people globally for HP's printing business because she revealed her potential during adversity.

The difference between Kevin and Anneliese isn't their courage, it's their starting point. Kevin proves you don't need to seek out adversity; it will find you. When it does, how you respond determines whether it breaks you or makes you. Anneliese proves that actively choosing challenges builds your capacity to handle the ones that choose you.

Aaron lost his legs to meningitis, imposed adversity at its most extreme. But then he chose to climb Kilimanjaro on his hands and knees. The pattern is clear: growth comes not from the adversity itself, but from how we choose to engage with it.

Both Kevin and Anneliese developed something essential for our AI age: comfort with operating in unfamiliar territory. Kevin learned to make high-stakes decisions from the available data, exactly what AI collaboration requires. Anneliese discovered she could become expert in something she initially knew nothing about, the growth mindset essential for keeping pace with AI advancement.

Whether adversity chooses you or you choose it, the result is the same: expanded capacity for handling uncertainty, faster learning cycles, and confidence that you can figure out what you don't yet know. These aren't just leadership skills, they're survival skills for thriving alongside AI.

TRY THIS: BUILDING YOUR ADVERSITY CAPACITY

Aaron, Kevin, and Anneliese each developed adversity capacity in different ways. Use their examples to assess your own readiness for life's inevitable challenges. As you rate yourself on each dimension, consider how each of our three protagonists would have scored at different points in their journeys.

YOUR ADVERSITY PROPRIOCEPTION ASSESSMENT
Rate yourself honestly (1–10 scale) across all six dimensions.

SELF-LEADERSHIP AWARENESS → INSPIRE
Internal Landscape Check

- How well do I understand my typical responses to adversity? ___/10

- Do I recognize my "dragons" (fears) before they over-whelm me? ___/10
- Can I choose my response rather than defaulting to a reaction under pressure? ___/10

Learn from Aaron: In that hospital bed, Aaron could have chosen victim thinking. Instead, he said, "Mum, I'm going to beat this." That moment of choosing his response, not his circumstances, set everything in motion.

Reflection Prompt: "When facing challenges, am I the author of my story or living someone else's script about what I 'should' do?"

COMPETENCE INTELLIGENCE → GUIDE
Skills Reality Check

- How accurately do I assess what I can actually handle right now? ___/10
- Do I know the difference between challenges that will grow me versus those that will break me? ___/10
- Can I identify what specific skills I need to develop for upcoming challenges? ___/10

Learn from Kevin: Kevin had been running operations for five years when crisis struck. His competence intelligence told him he had insights worth sharing, even if it meant risking his job. He knew what he could handle.

Reflection Prompt: "What's the hardest thing I've successfully navigated, and what capabilities did that reveal?"

Somatic Awareness → Nurture (Well-Being)
Body Wisdom Check

- Do I notice physical stress signals before they become overwhelming? ___/10
- Can I distinguish between "good stress" (growth) and "bad stress" (breakdown)? ___/10
- Do I have reliable methods for physical and emotional regulation? ___/10

Learn from Aaron: Crawling up Kilimanjaro, Aaron was "falling to bits" and "covered in blood." But he knew the difference between discomfort that builds character and damage that breaks you. His body was telling him to stop, his purpose was telling him to continue.

Reflection Prompt: "What does my body tell me about my capacity for challenge? Am I energized or depleted?"

Relational Intelligence → Nurture (Belonging)
Support System Assessment

- Do I have people who can help me navigate difficult situations? ___/10
- Can I ask for help without feeling like I'm failing? ___/10
- Do I know who to turn to for different types of support (practical, emotional, strategic)? ___/10

Learn from Anneliese: Alone in China, not speaking the language, Anneliese knew "there was no one else."

But she actively asked questions: "How do we go about doing this? What don't I know? How do I lean on others?" She built her support network by being vulnerable about what she didn't know.

Reflection Prompt: "Who has helped me through adversity before, and how can I strengthen those relationships?"

PURPOSE ALIGNMENT → TRANSFORM
Meaning-Making Capacity

- Can I find meaning and growth opportunities in difficult situations? ___/10
- Do my current challenges align with my deeper values and goals? ___/10
- Am I clear about what I'm building toward, not just what I avoid? ___/10

Learn from Kevin: Kevin could have seen Porsche's crisis as a threat to his comfortable operations role. Instead, he recognized it as alignment with his larger purpose, to lead, not just manage. The crisis wasn't derailing his career goals; it was accelerating them. By risking everything to tell the truth, he transformed from middle management to CEO because the challenge matched his deeper values of authentic leadership.

Reflection Prompt: "How do my current challenges serve my larger purpose, even if they are uncomfortable?"

INTEGRATION CAPACITY → INTEGRATE + EVALUATE
Adaptive Learning Check

- Do I learn from setbacks rather than just enduring them? ____/10
- Can I see patterns across different challenges I've faced? ____/10
- Do I actively seek tools and resources (including AI) to help me grow through difficulty? ____/10

Learn from Anneliese: Facing the China crisis, Anneliese didn't pretend to know what she didn't know. She integrated every available resource, her management skills, local teams, her boss's guidance, and systematic questioning, to become expert in an unfamiliar domain. "I used all my management, one-on-one, and business skills," she said. Two years later, she was the expert everyone turned to for complex problems because she'd learned to rapidly integrate new knowledge under pressure.

Reflection Prompt: "What pattern do I see across all these dimensions, and what needs the most attention?"

Total Adversity Proprioception Score: ____/60
Identify Your Growth Edge

- Which dimension scored lowest in your assessment?
- What pattern showed up most often in your reflections?
- Where do you feel most/least prepared for future challenges?

Create Your Adversity Action Plan
This month, I will strengthen my _____ dimension by:

- One specific action I'll take weekly
- One resource (person, tool, practice) I'll engage
- One way I'll measure progress

Set Your Challenge Intention
Complete this statement: "I'm ready to take on _____ challenge because my proprioceptive assessment shows I have _____ strengths and I'm developing _____ areas."

Remember: Mental toughness isn't about blind positivity or pretending challenges don't exist. It's about developing mental and emotional resources to perform at your best when it matters most. The stronger your mental toughness, the more potential you can access under pressure.

Personal resilience is essential, but human potential truly flourishes in community. As leaders, our greatest responsibility is creating environments where others can unlock their own potential.

PART III

WHAT INSPIRES EXCELLENCE IN OTHERS?

THE IMPACT

Here's the secret every great leader eventually discovers: your own potential multiplies when you unlock it in others.

I've watched this transformation hundreds of times. A manager struggling with their own confidence suddenly becomes magnetic when they start seeing potential in their team. A parent worried about their child's future finds peace when they learn to nurture instead of pressure. A teacher burned out by the system rediscovers their calling when they become a "potential whisperer" instead of an information deliverer.

This is where the real magic happens, where individual development becomes collective transformation, where your journey to potential becomes a movement that changes everything around you.

In Part III, you'll discover how to create what I call "Goldilocks Zones," environments where people feel safe enough to be vulnerable and challenged enough to grow.

You'll learn why the old command-and-control leadership is not just outdated but dangerous in an AI world, and what's taking its place.

We'll explore the profound power of belief and belonging, how the simple act of seeing someone's potential and helping them feel they belong can literally change the trajectory of their life. You'll meet Jessica Fontana, who left Meta to empower women leaders worldwide; Stevo Stephenson, who discovered that measuring well-being instead of boat speed produced both happier kids and faster boats; and leaders who learned that when you ignite others, you don't diminish yourself – you multiply your impact.

But this isn't about becoming everyone's motivational coach or fixing broken people. It's about something much more fundamental: creating conditions where human potential naturally emerges, like flowers turning toward sunlight.

The leaders who will shape the next decade won't be those who have the best relationship with AI, though that matters. They'll be the ones who remember that behind every algorithm is a human being with unlimited potential waiting to be awakened.

This is your chance to become what the world desperately needs: someone who doesn't just achieve their own potential but ignites it in others. Someone who creates ripples of possibility that spread far beyond what they can see.

In the end, the measure of a life well lived isn't what you accomplished; it's what you awakened in others.

Your potential is calling. But more importantly, so is theirs.

And that's where the real adventure begins.

CHAPTER 8

NOT TOO HOT, NOT TOO COLD: CREATING THE POTENTIALIZE ZONE

"This porridge is too hot! This porridge is too cold! This porridge is just right!"

– Robert Southey

Adversity reveals potential, but it is only unleashed when nurtured in the right environment. Aaron, Kevin, and Anneliese didn't just survive their challenges; they thrived because they found themselves in conditions that were demanding enough to force growth but supportive enough to prevent breaking. These optimal conditions don't have to be an accident when we understand what environments allow human potential to flourish naturally.

James "Stevo" Stephenson chose to create the right culture at the right time, changing lives in the process.

As the rowing director at a New Zealand school, he could have followed the traditional path, pushing harder, measuring boat speed, and celebrating only the winners. Or he could try something that sounded crazy to every other coach: stop measuring performance entirely.

When a group of girls approached Stevo after a tragic suicide at their school, they wanted to transform the culture through rowing. The traditional approach would be to measure boat speed, but being trained as a pastor, he chose seven completely different metrics: Are you eating better? Sleeping better? Doing better academically? Do you have more friends? Are you speaking to your parents better? Do you feel healthier? Are you happier?

Other coaches thought he had lost his mind, and parents worried their daughters weren't being pushed hard enough. But Stevo understood something profound about human potential: when you create the right environment, performance takes care of itself.

Every student and parent involved reported overwhelming joy and fulfillment. And the remarkable part is that they ended up beating everyone else. But they never measured boat speed. They just showed up saying, "We're going to have a fulfilling experience."

This is the Goldilocks Zone in action: not too much pressure, not too little challenge, but conditions just right for human potential to flourish naturally.

In astronomy, the Goldilocks Zone refers to the habitable region around a star where conditions are "just right" for liquid water to exist (not too hot and not too cold). Our planet Earth resides in such a Goldilocks Zone, making all life here possible.

Inspiring excellence also requires a Goldilocks environment. Ideally, it should not be so comfortable that people become complacent (like plants overwatered in a greenhouse developing shallow roots). Neither should people be so challenged that they break under pressure (like a seedling in harsh conditions that withers before it can establish itself).

In the ideal Goldilocks environment, people encounter just enough resistance to build strength and resilience but with sufficient support to prevent burnout or failure.

In our AI age, this principle becomes even more critical as we navigate new forms of human–machine collaboration. For example:

Challenge Calibration

- **Too Cold:** Letting AI handle everything while humans become passive observers.
- **Too Hot:** Forcing humans to compete directly with AI on speed and processing.
- **Just Right:** Using AI to handle routine tasks while humans focus on judgment, creativity, and complex problem-solving.

Learning and Development

- **Too Cold:** Relying entirely on AI without developing human capabilities.
- **Too Hot:** Overwhelming people with AI tools they can't understand or use effectively.
- **Just Right:** AI accelerates human learning by providing instant feedback, research support, and skill development opportunities.

Decision-Making Balance

- **Too Cold:** Blindly following AI recommendations without human oversight.
- **Too Hot:** Rejecting AI insights and making decisions purely on human intuition.
- **Just Right:** Combining AI's data processing with human wisdom, context, and ethical judgment.

Autonomy and Control

- **Too Cold:** Humans become dependent on AI for basic thinking.
- **Too Hot:** Humans resist AI collaboration entirely, missing productivity gains.
- **Just Right:** Humans maintain agency while leveraging AI as a powerful thinking partner.

Feedback and Growth

- **Too Cold:** AI provides all the answers, eliminating human problem-solving practice.

- **Too Hot:** Information overload from AI systems creates analysis paralysis.
- **Just Right:** AI provides just enough support to help humans stretch beyond current capabilities while building new competencies.

WHAT IS EXCELLENCE?

Who has inspired you? It was likely a teacher, a coach, an early manager, or a mentor. You were inspired toward excellence because somebody believed in you more than you believed in yourself.

Who do you inspire? Who has unlocked or uncovered their potential because you believed in them? This is your legacy.

Excellence resists simple definition because it operates simultaneously across multiple dimensions: performance, character, meaning, and impact. Unlike success (which can be measured externally) or achievement (which has clear endpoints), excellence is both process and outcome, individual and collective, temporal and timeless.

Inspiring excellence isn't just about measuring times, distances, or win–loss records. It's not about profits, market share, or stock price. And it's certainly not about the number of followers and likes on social media. These might be byproducts of excellence, but focusing only on the metrics will ultimately lead to burnout.

> "Excellence is not an act, but a habit. We are what we repeatedly do."
>
> – Aristotle

In Chapter 2, we explored the tension between Delphi's and Sparta's ideas and concluded that integrating both insights would be the wisest approach. Know yourself deeply enough to understand what you uniquely have to offer. Serve something larger than yourself that gives meaning and direction to your unique gift.

To inspire excellence, we must create a Goldilocks Zone that ignites autonomous motivation while providing guiding principles, a metaphorical safe sandbox for humans.

This section explores the kind of leadership and culture that will nurture the seeds of excellence.

THIS IS NOT SPARTA!

When each of my children was born, I was overcome with a flood of emotions and a desire to protect their precious lives at all costs. I could not imagine handing them over to the state, as in Ancient Sparta.

How could I balance support with the appropriate challenges for them to develop self-leadership and confident humility?

When my daughter Tasha turned 14, the COVID pandemic lockdowns separated us in different households. To stay connected, we played the 3D sandbox video game *Minecraft*. I was a complete novice, but I persevered because it was what she liked. (It was much easier with my son, as we both enjoyed chess.) I noticed that Tasha could upgrade her character's armor, but I didn't know how, and so I was repeatedly defeated by the zombies!

"Tasha, darling, could you upgrade my armor for me?" I asked her.

"I could, but then you wouldn't learn anything," she replied.

At that moment, I was a proud father. My daughter recognized the importance of autonomy in overcoming challenges. She was the driver, not the passenger.

In contrast, teachers and educators have told me about the challenges of dealing with helicopter parents, lawn mower parents, and jackhammer parents.

Helicopter parents hover over their children and interject themselves into their children's activities to protect them from harm. Lawnmower parents mow down any obstacle or potential danger in their child's path that could bring hardship or discomfort, and jackhammer parents scrutinize their children's opportunities and challenges, intervening in schooling, grades, and friendships.

As well-intentioned as these behaviors are, they are detrimental. Research has shown that over-parenting decreases self-reliance, resilience, and confidence, while increasing anxiety and depression. Children of lawnmower parents often have underdeveloped executive function skills like planning, prioritizing, and managing time since they've had limited practice.

MICROMANAGING SUCKS

There are strong parallels between parenting styles and poor people management.

Micromanaging bosses can destroy employees' sense of autonomy and professional confidence. This is so common that you probably have personal experience with it.

Under constant supervision, we are less likely to take initiative or make independent decisions.

Micromanaged employees demonstrate diminished problem-solving abilities over time. When managers consistently offer solutions or pre-emptively eliminate obstacles, employees miss opportunities to cultivate critical thinking skills and creative approaches to challenges.

Micromanaged employees report higher stress, anxiety, and burnout; they internalize the message that they aren't trusted to handle responsibilities independently.

While the intention may be to ensure high standards, children and employees in an environment of constant supervision tend to become risk-averse, have less innovative, and are more dependent on external validation.

Micromanaging sucks the potential out of children and adults alike.

Think of developing people like training them for a marathon. Push too hard and they get injured. Too easy, and they don't improve. The magic happens in that narrow band where they're challenged just enough to grow but not so much that they break.

Tennis coach Tim Gallwey discovered this principle accidentally. Initially, he focused on giving students traditional technical instructions, but he stopped teaching one day. To his amazement, students improved faster without his constant corrections.

PERFORMANCE EQUALS POTENTIAL MINUS INTERFERENCE

"Performance equals potential minus interference," Gallwey concluded (Gallwey, 1974). The primary obstacle to realizing potential isn't lack of ability but mental interference, the constant self-criticism, overthinking, and tension that well-meaning instruction can create.

Gallwey's insight revolutionizes how we think about creating environments for potential. Most leaders focus on what to add: more training, feedback, and structure. But often, the breakthrough comes from what you remove: the interference that prevents natural learning.

This is precisely what micromanaging creates: interference. When managers constantly supervise, correct, and direct, they generate the mental static that blocks flow states. Employees become self-conscious, second-guessing their instincts instead of trusting their developing competence.

The Goldilocks Zone isn't just about finding the right level of challenge. It's about creating conditions where interference is minimized and natural learning can emerge. Sometimes the most powerful thing a leader can do is step back and trust the process.

LEARNING FOR EXCELLENCE

But what does a perfect Goldilocks Zone look like in practice? A company in Romania's competitive car-leasing industry provides a remarkable example of how the right balance can transform both culture and performance.

The leadership team at this Romanian company made a decision that would have seemed absurd to most executives. Every employee, regardless of level or role, was required to read one book per month; not the same book, not business books selected by management, but any book the employee chose.

The company would provide the books. The only requirement was simple: to get a little bit better each month.

"The whole idea is that we are not reading the same business books," explained organizational culture expert Magor Csibi, who has worked closely with the company. "The diversity of all those ideas is generating a lot of new approaches, a lot of new procedures, a lot of new ideas in the organization."

What this company created was organizational alchemy, the precise balance that defines a Goldilocks Zone.

- **Challenge:** Every employee must expand their knowledge monthly, but they control how.
- **Support:** The company provides the books and creates time for learning discussions.
- **Autonomy:** Employees choose their own reading material and determine how to apply insights.
- **Purpose:** Individual growth serves collective innovation and market success.

The results spoke for themselves. The company evolved from a regional player to a dominant force in Romania's leasing and car rental market. But the real magic became visible in unexpected moments.

Magor witnessed the transformation firsthand while visiting one of their provincial headquarters. He was having lunch with a senior executive, discussing insights from a business book they had both read, when something extraordinary happened.

A worker from the car wash operation, sitting at the next table, overheard their conversation. When they finished eating and prepared to leave, the car wash worker approached them.

"Can I tell you what book I'm reading right now? And how I apply it in my everyday work?"

This wasn't a publicity stunt or staged encounter. This was the natural result of creating an environment where continuous learning became cultural DNA rather than a corporate mandate.

The Ripple Effect of Excellence

The company's Goldilocks Zone created something that no amount of traditional training could achieve: genuine psychological safety across all organizational levels. When learning becomes universal rather than hierarchical, several profound shifts occur.

- **Flattened Expertise:** Knowledge can come from anywhere, eliminating artificial barriers between "thinkers" and "doers."
- **Elevated Conversations:** "When everybody is learning, when everybody is curious about growing, the discussions, the level of discussions, the level of the challenge in an organization tends to look different."

- **Internal Mobility:** Most top managers were promoted from the first layer of the organization because the company became a talent development engine rather than just an operational business.

Then, something unexpected happened: people started joining the company specifically because they knew they would "learn quickly and get much better after working one or two years with them."

The company had accidentally created what researchers call "talent magnetism," where high-potential people actively seek out environments that accelerate their growth. They weren't just hiring employees but attracting people who saw their role as part of a larger development journey.

But reading alone didn't create this transformation. The company redesigned its organizational structure to be "very fluid," where "almost anybody can address anybody inside the organization to generate ideas."

This wasn't anarchy, it was intentional architecture. They created clear goals and outcomes while allowing maximum flexibility in how people achieved them.

The Romanian company demonstrates what happens when organizations stop treating human development as an expense and start viewing it as a source of competitive advantage. They didn't just improve their financial performance; they created a fundamentally different workplace where potential naturally emerges.

The Goldilocks Principle in Practice

What makes this story particularly powerful is how it illustrates the delicate balance required for sustainable excellence.

- **Too Cold (The Spartan Way):** Traditional hierarchical companies where only senior executives are expected to contribute strategic thinking.
- **Too Hot (The Delphi Way):** Chaotic environments with no structure or clear expectations.
- **Just Right:** Clear outcomes with maximum autonomy in methods, universal learning expectations, and fluid communication structures.

The Romanian company found its sweet spot by trusting that when you combine high expectations with high support, people don't just meet expectations, they exceed them in ways you never imagined.

This is what organizational potential looks like when unleashed rather than managed, nurtured rather than controlled, and trusted rather than micromanaged.

The Science of Social Learning

The Romanian company's success proves what psychologist Mihaly Csikszentmihalyi discovered: when challenge perfectly matches skill level, people enter "flow" – a state where time disappears and performance soars. But flow isn't just individual; it's contagious in the right environment.

Think about the last time you were completely absorbed in work. Hours felt like minutes. You weren't thinking about yourself or checking your phone. You were simply. . . there, fully present and capable.

Flow occurs when three conditions align: **challenge level** matches your current abilities; **clear goals** with immediate feedback; and **complete focus** without distractions. The Romanian company created these conditions through their reading program, but the real magic happened in their social learning spaces.

As Anupama Lal, Head of Learning and Culture at KPMG Asia Pacific, explains: "Learning isn't a solitary experience. I focus on creating social learning opportunities where people talk about what they're learning, what they're finding useful, and what's challenging. People want to understand what others are doing; almost to feel they're not alone in whatever they're grappling with."

This mirrors what the Ancient Greeks understood when they used the word "school," from *scholē*, meaning "leisure." Education was social, occurring in marketplaces where ideas could cross-pollinate. Today, we have unprecedented access to information through Google and AI, but we still need social spaces to transform information into wisdom.

This wisdom becomes critical when leading in the AI age. We used to laugh at people who drove into ponds following GPS directions. Now we might drive off a cliff if we don't engage our humanity and critical thinking when partnering with AI.

The leaders of the Romanian car-leasing company succeeded because they understood that creating a Goldilocks Zone requires both vision and execution. They didn't just declare "we value learning"; they built systems, allocated resources, and measured what mattered. But what happens when leaders have the right intentions but miss the execution entirely?

WHEN GOOD INTENTIONS MEET POOR EXECUTION

Steve Cadigan, LinkedIn's first Chief HR Officer, once worked with a young Canadian tech company whose founders had the right aspirations but completely missed the execution. The story serves as a cautionary tale about the difference between declaring intentions and creating actual conditions for potential to flourish.

Both founders, in their early thirties, approached Steve with unbridled enthusiasm: "Steve, we want to be the best company in the world to work for remotely."

It sounded impressive. Remote work was gaining momentum, top talent was scattered globally, and being "the best" at anything seemed like a worthy goal. But when Steve asked the obvious follow-up question, the conversation took an interesting turn.

"Great," Steve replied. "How will you know if you've achieved that goal? Like, what's happening? How will you know that you've realized that outcome?"

"Complete deer in the headlights," Steve recalls. "Like what? Like, yeah. Don't know, didn't have an answer for that."

The founders had confused aspiration with strategy. They wanted to attract Silicon Valley talent to their Canadian company and figured that being "fully remote" would be their competitive advantage. But they had never actually seen remote work succeed at scale, had no metrics for measuring "best," and no framework for creating the conditions that would make remote collaboration thrive.

Steve pressed further: "Are you setting that as an objective because you believe that will make you more attractive to hard-to-hire candidates?"

The answer was yes, they had a thesis, but it was untested. They were building a new company, going through the natural growing pains of organizational "puberty," and simultaneously conducting a massive experiment with their entire operating model.

"It was a great aspiration," Steve reflects, "but you've never seen it work. You don't know how it could work. You know, it's a big gamble and you're building a new company."

Three years later, the experiment had failed. The founders were quietly abandoning their remote-first approach: "You need to have centers of excellence. We all need to be together. It's not working. Communication's poor."

What went wrong? They had violated every principle of creating a Goldilocks Zone.

Too Cold: They hired very junior leaders, without experience, navigating remote team dynamics. Without strong communication skills and systems thinking, the distributed team couldn't create the psychological safety needed for excellence.

Too Hot: They threw people into a completely new way of working without the infrastructure, training, or support systems to succeed. It was like asking someone to perform gymnastics without teaching them how to land safely.

No "Just Right": They never defined what success looked like, never measured progress against meaningful metrics, and never adjusted their approach based on feedback. They were flying blind in conditions that required precise navigation.

The irony? The business itself began struggling, not because remote work is inherently flawed, but because they had confused a work arrangement with a business strategy. They had focused entirely on where people worked without addressing how they worked together.

"They didn't invest a lot in communication and understanding the value of that," Steve notes. "And so it was an interesting thought experiment, but it never actualized."

This story illustrates a crucial point about creating environments for potential: good intentions aren't enough. The Goldilocks Zone requires deliberate design, continuous measurement, and the wisdom to know the difference between what sounds good and what actually works.

The Canadian founders learned an expensive lesson that many organizations are still learning: you cannot optimize for potential by changing only the location of work.

You must optimize for the conditions that allow human beings to do their best thinking, create meaningful relationships, and grow beyond what they thought possible.

Creating the perfect environment for potential isn't about finding the one right answer. it's about building systems that can adapt and improve based on real feedback from real people doing real work. The founders had the vision but missed the execution. In the Goldilocks Zone, both matter equally.

THE ENVIRONMENT FOR EXCELLENCE

Enjoyment emerges when the balance between individual potential and environmental conditions is right. With the correct conditions, you witness intrinsic motivation.

Ruth Gotian, author of *The Success Factor* (Gotian, 2022) and Chief Learning Officer at Weill Cornell Medicine, told me: "Extrinsic motivation means you're doing it for the Nobel Prize, the Olympic medal, the bonus, the diploma on the wall. That's fleeting because that's when other people are judging you. And what do you do after you get that award?

Do you quit? But if it comes from within, that's the fire in your belly. That's what's keeping you up at night. This is the reason you can't quiet your mind because you're always thinking about it. You always want to do better. You're always looking at the film to see what things you can improve to be faster, stronger, better, and more efficient.

These are the types of things you do when you're intrinsically motivated. And I think if we can tap into that, we can reach the potential."

Management guru Peter Drucker famously said, "Culture eats strategy for breakfast." This chapter examines the principles required to create a Goldilocks Zone, a culture that unlocks potential.

There is No Gene for the Human Spirit

When we see talent, we can be tempted to force excellence. In the 1950s and 1960s, the Soviet Union created a talent identification system for young gymnasts. Just as Sparta took young boys from their parents, children as young as seven were taken from their families and sent to live in training centers. Their whole life became a "push for victory," with pursuing a gold medal being "non-negotiable."

The system was highly effective at producing champions but had significant costs. The competition was fierce, with only a select few chosen to compete at the highest levels, which created intense pressure for both athletes and coaches. This pressure sometimes led to coaches abusing their power and intimidating gymnasts before elite competitions.

Gattaca (1997) is a science fiction film directed by Andrew Niccol. It explores a dystopian future in which genetic engineering has created a society divided between the genetically enhanced "valid" and naturally conceived "invalid."

The film's famous line, "There is no gene for the human spirit," encapsulates its core message: human potential cannot be quantified or predetermined, and the essential human qualities remain beyond measurement.

TRY THIS: THE GOLDILOCKS ZONE CREATOR

Use the IGNITE framework to create conditions for potential to flourish naturally.

INSPIRE: SPARK THE RIGHT CULTURE

Weekly Culture Check: Ask your team this simple question: "Are you energized or drained by your current challenges?"
Listen for three signals.

- **Too Cold:** "It's boring"/"I could do this in my sleep"/"I'm not learning anything"
- **Too Hot:** "I'm overwhelmed"/"I can't keep up"/ "Everything feels urgent"
- **Just Right:** "Time flies when I'm working"/"I feel stretched but capable"/"I'm growing"

Your Goldilocks Inspiration: Complete this sentence: "I want to create an environment where my team. . ."

GUIDE: NAVIGATE THE BALANCE

Individual Calibration

Ask three diagnostic questions.

1. **Challenge Level:** "On a scale of 1–10, how challenged do you feel right now?" (Target: 6–8)
2. **Support Level:** "How supported do you feel when facing difficulties?" (Target: 7–9)

3. **Growth Direction:** "What's the next capability you want to develop?"

Adjustment Actions

- If Challenge < 6: Add responsibility, complexity, or stretch projects.
- If Challenge > 8: Provide more support, break down tasks, or temporarily reduce scope.
- If Support < 7: Increase check-ins, provide resources, or remove obstacles.

NURTURE: BUILD BELIEF AND BELONGING

Psychological Safety Assessment

Rate your team environment (1–5 scale):

- People admit mistakes without fear ____
- Ideas are welcomed, even imperfect ones ____
- Everyone feels their voice matters ____
- Risk-taking is encouraged and supported ____
- Learning from failure is celebrated ____

Belonging Builders

- **Weekly:** Recognize someone's unique contribution publicly
- **Monthly:** Share how individual growth serves team goals
- **Quarterly:** Celebrate progress, not just achievements

INTEGRATE: COMBINE HUMAN + AI EXCELLENCE

Technology as Flow Enabler

Ask yourself: "How can AI tools help my team reach flow states more easily?"

Examples:

- Use AI to handle routine tasks, freeing time for meaningful work.
- Let AI provide instant feedback so people don't wait for guidance.
- Have AI analyze patterns to help you spot "too hot" or "too cold" signals.

Human + AI Balance Check

- What work requires human judgment, creativity, or connection?
- What tasks could AI handle to eliminate interference?
- How can technology amplify rather than replace human capabilities?

TRANSFORM: TURN CHALLENGES INTO GROWTH

The Goldilocks Challenge Ladder

For each team member, identify the following.

1. **Current Comfort Zone:** What they do easily.
2. **Stretch Zone:** What challenges them appropriately (their 7/10).
3. **Stress Zone:** What would overwhelm them (their 9–10).

Progressive Challenge Design

- Start challenges in their 6–7 range
- Provide support to prevent slipping into stress zone
- Gradually increase difficulty as competence grows

Failure as Learning: When someone struggles, ask: "What did this teach us about finding your optimal challenge level?"

EVALUATE: Measure What Matters
Monthly Goldilocks Metrics

Track the following three indicators.

1. **Flow Frequency:** "How often did you lose track of time while working this month?"
2. **Energy Direction:** "Are you more energized or depleted than last month?"
3. **Growth Evidence:** "What new capability did you develop?"

Team Environment Pulse

Quick monthly team survey (three questions):

- "How would you rate your challenge–support balance?" (1–10)
- "Do you feel psychologically safe to take risks?" (Yes/No)
- "What one change would improve your Goldilocks Zone?"

Adjustment Protocol

- Green Zone (7–9 average): Maintain current approach.
- Yellow Zone (5–6 average): Investigate and adjust within two weeks.
- Red Zone (1–4 average): Emergency recalibration needed.

Remember: Your job isn't to be perfect at this immediately. Like Goldilocks herself, you will need to test, adjust, and find what's "just right" for each unique individual on your team. The magic happens when people feel simultaneously stretched and supported.

Creating the right environment requires a new kind of leadership, one that can navigate the complexity of human–AI collaboration while maintaining the essentially human elements of trust, meaning, and connection.

CHAPTER 9

THE POWER OF BELIEF AND BELONGING

"A hero is someone who has given his or her life to something bigger than oneself"

– Joseph Campbell

What transforms adversity into advantage? What makes the difference between a Goldilocks Zone that merely functions and one that ignites extraordinary performance? The answer isn't found in better systems or optimal challenge ratios. It's found in something far more fundamental and mysteriously powerful: belief.

Aaron didn't crawl up Kilimanjaro alone – he carried the belief of coaches who saw champion potential in a man who'd lost his legs. The Romanian company's reading program didn't succeed because of books – it worked because leaders believed every employee, from executives to car wash workers, had wisdom worth sharing.

In our rush to create perfect environments and navigate challenges, we often overlook the invisible force that makes everything else possible: the moment when someone believes in potential that hasn't yet been proven, and people discover they belong to something larger than themselves.

An inspirational example of belief defying logic happened on a Caribbean island in the 1980s, when two Americans looked at Jamaican sprinters and saw something no one else could imagine: Olympic bobsledders.

Cool Runnings (Walt Disney Pictures 1993) is a heartwarming story about the power of belief and belonging. The movie is loosely based on the debut of the Jamaican national bobsleigh team at the 1988 Winter Olympics in Calgary, Canada.

Two Americans, George Fitch (a businessman) and William Maloney (who had spent time in Jamaica), saw an opportunity for a Jamaican bobsleigh team. They believed that the pushing power of Jamaican sprinters could effectively translate to bobsleigh starts.

Unlike the movie portrayal, the original team members weren't failed Olympic track athletes who couldn't compete in summer events. Most were members of the Jamaica Defense Force, though Devon Harris had competed as a middle-distance runner. Dudley Stokes was a helicopter pilot, and Chris Stokes (his brother) was a university track athlete who joined the team at the last minute.

The true story is about belief, determination, and belonging (representing their country in a completely foreign sport). The team had less than a year to train for an extremely technical winter sport they had never seen before, coming from a tropical island.

They crashed during one of their four runs in their Olympic debut and did not officially finish the competition. However, they earned tremendous respect from the bobsleigh community and spectators worldwide for their courage and determination.

The opportunity for participation broke barriers and inspired other tropical nations to compete in winter sports. The real achievement was showing that geographic limitations didn't have to restrict athletic participation.

Jamaica has since become a legitimate competitor in the sport, qualifying for several subsequent Winter Olympics and achieving respectable results.

In an age when AI can process data and optimize outcomes, what the Jamaican bobsleigh team discovered remains irreplaceable: the human forces of belief and belonging that transform impossible dreams into reality. These aren't just feel-good concepts; they are psychological foundations that determine whether people thrive alongside AI or get replaced by it.

THE SCIENCE OF BELIEF

A belief is an idea or thought validated or reinforced, resulting in a worldview.

Once we believe something, such as that our sports team is the best, we will reject any evidence to the contrary. This is because beliefs become neurologically embedded, filtering what we notice and ignore. Our brain uses beliefs as predictors for future performance.

When Henry Ford said, "If you think you can, you can; if you think you can't, you can't; either way, you are correct," he was stating an observable truth backed up by neuroscience.

But what happens when somebody believes in you?

The Ancient Greek myth of Pygmalion tells the story of a sculptor from Cyprus who creates a statue of a woman so beautiful and ideal that he falls in love with it. In Ovid's version, Pygmalion's love for the statue of his creation is so profound that during the festival of Venus (Aphrodite), he prays to the goddess to bring his creation to life. Venus grants his wish, and the statue comes to life under his touch.

George Bernard Shaw cleverly adapts this myth in his 1913 play, transforming it into a commentary on social class, education, and identity in early 20th-century London. Shaw's Pygmalion and the later musical *My Fair Lady* feature Henry Higgins, a phonetics professor who bets that he can transform a Cockney flower seller, Eliza Doolittle, into someone who can pass for a duchess in high society by teaching her proper speech and manners.

The myth and Shaw's play deal with transforming and unleashing potential through self-belief.

The Pygmalion effect, also known as the Rosenthal effect, is a fascinating psychological phenomenon in which belief leads to improved performance. In 1968, Robert Rosenthal and Lenore Jacobson went into a school and told teachers that certain students were about to have breakthrough years, real "growth spurters" based on a spe-cial test. The twist? There was no test. They had picked the kids randomly.

By the end of the year, those randomly selected students actually did perform better. Not because they were smarter, but because their teachers unconsciously treated them like they were destined for success. The teachers gave them more attention, more challenging questions, and more encourage-ment. And the kids rose to meet those expectations.

Think about it: the teachers thought they were just teaching normally. But when you believe someone has potential, you can't help but interact with them differently. You lean in a little more. You wait a little longer for their answer. You see their mistakes as stepping stones rather than proof that they can't do it.

The students felt that belief, and it changed everything.

In another study, Israeli Defense Force soldiers in train-ing were randomly assigned to instructors who were told that their group had either high or average potential (Eden & Shani, 1982).

Soldiers believed to have high potential scored signifi-cantly better in their performance assessments. The Pyg-malion effect influenced leadership training and trainee performance in a military setting.

This power of belief shows up everywhere, even in fic-tional leaders who capture our imagination. Ted Lasso, the optimistic American coach in the hit Apple TV+ series, understood something profound about igniting potential.

"What about the belief of hope? Yeah, that's what I want to mess with, believing that things can get better, that I can get better, that we will get better. . . to believe in yourself, to believe in one another, man, that's fundamental to being alive."

Beliefs impact our behaviors toward others. Figure 9.1 shows the impact of these behaviors.

This effect's importance in developing potential cannot be overstated. It has profound implications across multiple domains and disciplines.

Teachers who believe in their students' capabilities create environments that foster growth and achievement. Students internalize these expectations and often rise to meet them.

Managers who communicate high expectations to their teams see improved performance and innovation. Employees who feel their potential is recognized tend to take more initiative and show greater creativity.

In the age of AI, it will be interesting to see whether the agents we partner with will have the same amplifying effect when they express their belief in us.

Encouraging Behaviors	Results of the Pygmalion Effect
• Providing more detailed feedback	1. Develop higher self-expectations
• Offering more challenging opportunities	2. Put forth greater effort
• Giving individuals more time to respond to questions	3. Persist longer in the face of challenges
• Maintaining a warmer and more supportive emotional climate	4. Take on more challenging tasks

Figure 9.1   The Pygmalion Effect

The Foundation of Belonging

If belief says, "You can do this," and belonging says, "You fit here," when both are present, potential is unleashed.

Ubuntu, a Southern African philosophy, captures something essential about belonging. The word comes from the Zulu phrase meaning "a person can only be a person through others." As Archbishop Desmond Tutu explained: "Ubuntu is the essence of being human."

This philosophy shaped Nelson Mandela's approach to post-apartheid reconciliation and Doc Rivers' strategy when coaching the 2008 Celtics to their championship. Rivers told his superstar players: "You're going to have to change. It's not about who is the best; it's about being the best for the team."

If you have ever seen the New Zealand All Blacks rugby team perform their traditional Māori Haka before a game, you have witnessed the embodiment of belief, and the team captures the idea of belonging with the mantra:

"Nobody is more important than the jersey"

The Haka and black jersey represent their relentless pursuit of excellence. Generations of players have worn the jersey with pride, multiplying individual potential through collective belonging.

With a win rate of over 76% across hundreds of Test matches, the All Blacks are the most successful international men's rugby team of all time through the combination of belief and belonging.

A sense of belonging profoundly shapes human potential and excellence across multiple dimensions of life. Communities of excellence – whether artistic movements, scientific disciplines, or athletic traditions – come together as sources of inspiration that establish collective standards and aspirations. When people feel they truly belong within a community, team, or organization, they can access deeper reserves of creativity, resilience, and performance.

THE PAIN OF EXCLUSION

In contrast, if you have ever been excluded from a group, you will know what research has discovered: your brain processes that rejection the same way it processes physical pain. The same neural pathways that fire when you break your arm also fire when someone gives you the cold shoulder at work or leaves you out of the group chat.

Your brain can't tell the difference between social pain and physical pain because, from an evolutionary perspective, being cast out from the tribe was often a death sentence.

This is why psychological safety is essential. When people feel they don't belong, their brains send danger signals. They're not going to be creative, take risks, or unlock their potential when their nervous system thinks they're under threat.

Teams where members feel they belong demonstrate higher job performance, reduced turnover, and decreased sick days. Employees who feel they belong are more likely to recommend their company as a great place to work.

BELIEF AND BELONGING COMBINED

I interviewed Caryn Davies, who won gold rowing medals at the 2008 and 2012 Olympics. Her journey to excellence began with a moment of belief in a supermarket.

At 12 years old and already nearly six feet tall, Caryn was shopping with her father when the local rowing coach spotted her. This big, gruff stranger strode up purposefully and declared, "I want you for rowing."

Terrified, Caryn hid behind her father. But the coach saw potential she didn't know she had; her height was a natural advantage for rowing. More importantly, he believed enough to recruit her.

"I took to it quickly and had some early success," Caryn recalls, "but what really clinched it for me was that I felt like I belonged. Rowing is a team sport, and I had teammates who wanted me in their boat and wanted me around. That was the first time I really felt that sense of belonging because I was quite an awkward teenager."

Notice the progression: belief (coach saw her potential) + belonging (teammates wanted her) = excellence. Caryn's potential was ignited not just by someone who believed in her capabilities, but by finding a community where she felt she belonged.

It's great when people believe in you, but sometimes you have to believe in yourself before you can belong.

Peggy Annette Whitson was born in Mount Ayr, Iowa, on February 9, 1960, and grew up on a farm. She developed an early interest in science, particularly after watching the Apollo moon landings as a child.

She pursued her education in biochemistry, earning a BSc from Iowa Wesleyan College in 1981 and a PhD in Biochemistry from Rice University in 1985. Before joining NASA, she worked as a research biochemist at the Johnson Space Center, focusing on the biochemistry of human adaptation to spaceflight.

Dr. Peggy Whitson was both willing and capable of being an astronaut, yet she was not given the opportunity. She repeatedly applied for training, over a period of 10 years, and faced rejection on each occasion.

She shared her mindset with Ruth Gotian. "There's something that they want that they're not seeing yet. The question is not whether I will become an astronaut. The question is how and when. What must I do to prove I have what they're looking for?"

People like Peggy, if you tell them the rules of the game, they will follow them and even exceed them. The problem is when the rules change.

In 1996, NASA selected Dr. Whitson as an astronaut candidate. After completing her training, she served in various technical roles before her first spaceflight (2002) as a flight engineer for Expedition 5 to the International Space Station (ISS). Her NASA career includes numerous groundbreaking achievements:

- She became the first female commander of the ISS during Expedition 16 in 2007–2008.
- She has broken multiple records for American astronauts, including the most cumulative time in space (665 days), most spacewalks by a woman (10), and most cumulative spacewalk time for a woman.

- At age 57, she became the oldest female astronaut in space.
- She served as the first female Chief of the Astronaut Office from 2009 to 2012.

Whitson's research in space has focused on areas including human adaptation to the space environment, microorganisms found on the ISS, and various biological experiments.

The lesson is that sometimes you must first believe in yourself before others do, but belonging validates that belief.

BEWARE THE DARK SIDE

Belief and belonging are powerful forces for unlocking potential, but like any powerful tool, they can be weaponized. The same psychological principles that created Olympic champions and championship teams can be perverted to exploit rather than develop people. Understanding this dark side helps us recognize when we're being developed versus when we're being used.

WeWork's collapse reveals exactly how the IGNITE framework can be weaponized when leaders prioritize their own agenda over genuine human development.

Adam Neumann masterfully corrupted each element of the IGNITE framework, creating the illusion of potential development while systematically exploiting his workforce.

INSPIRE (Corrupted): Neumann sold grandiose fantasy instead of authentic purpose. He promised employees they would "elevate the world's consciousness" through

shared workspace, transforming them from office workers into "architects of the future." This wasn't inspiring
growth; it was manufacturing delusion disconnected
from the reality of subletting desks.

GUIDE (Manipulated): Rather than mentoring toward
genuine capability, Neumann provided direction that
served only his enrichment. Employees were guided to
work 80-hour weeks for below-market salaries while
being told this sacrifice was "hustling for humanity."
True guidance develops people; Neumann's guidance
depleted them.

NURTURE (Exploited): WeWork created artificial
belonging through company retreats that resembled
religious revivals, complete with tequila shots and mes-
sianic speeches. But this wasn't psychological safety, it
was isolation. Employees were discouraged from outside
relationships that might provide perspective, creating
dependency rather than genuine community.

INTEGRATE (Perverted): Instead of combining human
potential with resources for mutual benefit, WeWork
extracted value from employees while Neumann cashed
out hundreds of millions personally. The integration served
only upward wealth transfer, not collaborative growth.

TRANSFORM (Hijacked): WeWork positioned every
challenge as a world-changing urgency, preventing careful
evaluation. Employees were told that questioning business fundamentals showed a lack of "cultural fit." True
transformation requires honest assessment; WeWork
demanded blind faith.

EVALUATE (Suppressed): When the Initial Public Offering filing revealed $5 billion in annual losses, the evaluation was devastating. Employees realized they had sacrificed their potential for someone else's enrichment. As one former employee told *Fast Company*: "Finding out it was just about making Adam rich while we worked ourselves to death. That broke something in me."

WeWork's $47 billion to $8 billion valuation collapse within months demonstrates what happens when IGNITE elements serve manipulation rather than development. Each framework element was present but corrupted:

- Inspiration became delusion
- Guidance became exploitation
- Nurturing became isolation
- Integration became extraction
- Transformation became manipulation
- Evaluation was suppressed until collapse was inevitable

The Lesson: When someone asks you to sacrifice your potential for their vision, evaluate whether the IGNITE framework is developing you or using you. True potential development creates mutual benefit; manipulation creates one-way extraction.

ONE MORE CAUTIONARY TALE

Dalia Feldheim, a former Chief Marketing Officer, told me about two experiences that illustrate the light and the dark side.

"I studied psychology and business and started with Procter Gamble in 1998. I was fortunate because P&G is a company that puts some money where the mouth is on maximizing human potential.

I had bosses who believed in me more than I believed in myself. So, it was always about what's the next great idea. You're in the driver's seat of your career. There was full flexibility and autonomy to build your own potential and others' potential.

After 17 years in PNG, having worked in Geneva, Moscow, and Singapore, I moved to another company as the CMO of Asia. It was a great company; everything seemed perfect, and it was a dream role.

One month into the role, I got a new boss, and he was a bully. I can't put it in nicer terms. He had a lot of issues himself, and he very strongly believed that the only way to succeed was by bringing other people down. He told me that very openly, and in many ways, I found it out.

It was a challenging time, and even though I had a very strong core, knew my values, and had potential, I started feeling like an impostor.

My strengths were not important to him. I was good with my people, driven, and positive, but in one meeting, he called me 'Miss Kumbaya,' which became my nickname.

One day, he brought me into his room and gave me feedback. I love feedback, even tough love because you talk about potential.

I believe that leaders shouldn't sugarcoat anything, right? You need to be honest. My previous managers and leaders had always come from a powerful sense of love. I'm with you; let's figure this out.

There was no love that day. It was really denigrating and humiliating. It was almost like he was on a mission. Later, I understood the mission. Then he started to insult my team, who worked hard and were important to me, and a tear appeared in my eye. He then smiled, and he gave me a box of tissues. I noticed something weird in his smile; he then turned around the tissue box he had given me, and on the other side was a sticker that said, 'Dalia's tissue box.'"

Shortly after this, Dalia left the company. And shortly after that, her boss was let go.

Fortunately, Dalia rediscovered her potential and strength before this experience because the damage could have been irreparable if this had been her first boss. Instead, Dalia is potentializing her experience as an author, speaker, and consultant.

Dalia survived the dark side because she had the experience of being believed in and being the driver of her own life in her first role. She reflected that she could have been destroyed if she had worked for the toxic boss before she developed autonomy.

CREATING BELIEF AND BELONGING THROUGH STORIES

What defines us as humans is our storytelling. Stories inspire us, inform us, and guide us.

Throughout this book, I have shared inspiring stories of people who have put their potential into action, even in the face of adversity.

Neuroscience research (Stephens, 2010) demonstrates that storytelling creates "neural coupling." When someone tells a story, the listener's brain activity mirrors that of the storyteller, creating a deep emotional connection and motivation.

An often-used example of the power of storytelling is when Steve Jobs introduced the iPhone to the world. He didn't lead with technical specifications; instead, he shared the story of three revolutionary products merging into one – an iPod, phone, and internet device. This narrative framework made the innovative product feel inevitable and inspiring.

Whether a parent, teacher, coach, manager, or leader, you must develop your storytelling to ignite the spark and inspire excellence.

THE HERO'S JOURNEY

Mythologist Joseph Campbell identified a universal transformation story structure that appears across all cultures: the hero's journey. Think of Frodo in *The Lord of The Rings*, Neo in *The Matrix*, or Luke in *Star Wars*.

Each hero is pulled from their ordinary world by a call to adventure. They meet a mentor and face tests and trials. Eventually, they face their deepest fear but survive with newfound insights and strengths that they can share with the world.

This same framework maps to our professional development.

- **Ordinary World:** Your current role feels routine, your potential untapped.

- **Call to Adventure:** A challenge appears that could unlock new capabilities (promotion opportunity, career change, new technology to master).
- **Initial Refusal:** "I'm not ready," "I don't have the skills," "What if I fail?"
- **Meeting the Mentor:** Someone believes in your potential and provides guidance (this could be a person, book, or even AI tool used wisely).
- **Crossing the Threshold:** You commit to the challenge despite fear or uncertainty.
- **Tests and Trials:** You develop new competencies while facing setbacks.
- **The Transformation:** You discover capabilities you didn't know you had.
- **Return with Wisdom:** You help others unlock their potential.

Practical application: Think of your biggest professional growth moment. Notice how it followed this pattern? The framework isn't just storytelling, it's a roadmap for intentional development.

As a Leader

- Identify where each team member is in their journey.
- Provide appropriate support for their current stage.
- Help them see challenges as "calls to adventure" rather than threats.
- Position yourself as the mentor who believes in their next level.

Your Current Journey Check

- What "call to adventure" are you currently avoiding?
- Who could serve as your mentor for this challenge?
- How could you be the mentor for someone else's journey?

Nick Jonsson, author of *Executive Loneliness*, exemplifies this journey. His ordinary world was a successful executive life until redundancy during his wife's pregnancy became his "call." He initially refused by putting on a "smiling face" and avoiding the issues.

At his lowest point, with severe health issues, anxiety, depression, and alcohol dependency, mentors appeared, including a support group that provided belonging and a new partner who believed in him. He crossed the threshold by stopping drinking and rebuilding physically through Ironman training.

His reward was emotional honesty and clear purpose: helping others overcome executive loneliness. Today, with some mentoring from me, he is an in-demand keynote speaker; he returns with the elixir of his hard-won wisdom.

Corporate Stories Work Too: Netflix's journey from DVD-by-mail to streaming giant follows the same pattern, from ordinary competitor to industry transformer through belief in streaming's potential, guidance from Blockbuster's failure, trials of content creation, and ultimately returning with the elixir of revolutionized entertainment.

MEETING THE MENTOR

Campbell's framework reveals that excellence isn't just about achieving goals; it's about becoming the person capable of achieving them. The journey transforms not just what you can do but who you are.

The catalyst for this transformation is a meeting with a mentor. This mentor can be an idea, a book, or an experience, but is usually a person who sees your potential and guides you toward performance and excellence.

Depending on where you are on your own hero's journey, you might need a mentor or be a mentor. Are you:

- Someone who has experience in a specific field or expertise?
- Someone interested in developing others?
- Someone prepared to take another by the hand and guide them on their journey?
- Someone who asks questions people don't ask themselves but ought to?
- Someone trustworthy who inspires confidence?

If you answered "Yes" to some or all of these questions, then you are a mentor or ready to become one.

MENTORING SKILLS

Being an effective mentor requires seven core skills that work together to create transformation. In the past, I would have argued that these are uniquely human skills, but I have been trialing increasingly sophisticated AI tools that do a

good job at many of these. We must remember the cautionary tale from Klarna in Chapter 1.

If AI cannot replace a human mentor, it could undoubtedly be a useful accelerator in training mentoring skills.

Here are the seven mentoring skills.

1. **Supporting:** Create psychological safety where mentees
   can share talents, challenges, fears, and aspirations. Trust
   is essential, reinforce it through confidentiality and positive intention.

2. **Listening:** Hear not just what is said, but how it's said
   and what isn't said. Effective listening receives, con-
   structs meaning, and responds to both verbal and non-
   verbal messages.

3. **Questioning:** Ask questions to help mentees gain clarity
   about their situation, inner dialogues, and choices, not
   for your own information, but for their insight.

4. **Reframing:** When you understand their inner world,
   ask "Does this serve you?" If not, help them reframe the
   situation as valuable learning on their hero's journey.

5. **Feedback:** Provide non-judgmental, factual observations
   that invite mentees to consider the impact of their behaviors. Effective feedback leads to informed choices about
   future actions.

6. **Celebration:** Because you know their journey, you're
   positioned to cheer them on as comfort zones stretch and
   achievements are reached.

7. **Guidance:** Judiciously share domain knowledge or connections. Mentoring isn't telling someone what to do; it's
   supporting them in finding their own path.

Research shows mentoring accelerates professional development and increases salary potential. At Sun Microsystems, mentored employees were promoted five times more often, while mentors were promoted six times more often. Sodexo found a 128% return on investment through employee retention and increased productivity.

Despite these benefits, according to Andy Lopata, who co-authored the *Financial Times Guide to Mentoring* with Ruth Gotian, only 37% of professionals have mentors because mentoring isn't front-and-center in organizational culture. We need to address this if we're serious about inspiring excellence.

Whether you're seeking a mentor or ready to become one, remember: excellence transforms not just what you can do, but who you are. The catalyst for this transformation is often a meeting with someone who sees your potential and guides you toward performance and excellence.

My first mentoring experience was with Radu, a Romanian intern who asked me, "How can I be like you in the shortest time possible?" I focused on developing his professional skills and judgment. When his parents visited Singapore, his father said, "Thank you for taking our boy and returning him as a man." Today, Radu runs a successful global recruitment firm. The transformation wasn't about copying me, it was about him discovering his own potential through guidance and belief.

Mentoring is a transformative process for both the mentee and the mentor. I experience personal and professional growth each time I mentor someone to unlock their potential, maximize their performance, and inspire excellence. If you haven't already, I encourage you to hone your mentoring skills.

WHY DON'T WE ASK FOR HELP?

The hero's journey reveals something crucial about human development: no hero succeeds alone. Luke had Obi-Wan, Frodo had Gandalf, Neo had Morpheus, and every real-world transformation story includes the moment when someone accepts help from others. Yet we resist this essential step.

Our personal and professional communities are the most significant resources outside of our own self-efficacy, but we are often reluctant to ask for help or input. Why do we struggle with what every hero's journey teaches us is necessary?

I asked Andy Lopata, an expert, about this because he is the author of the book *Just Ask: Why Seeking Support is your Greatest Strength* (Lopata, 2020).

"I think there are three main reasons we don't ask for help. Number one is we don't want to be a burden to other people. Number two is we don't want to be seen as vulnerable. Number three is we assume people can't or won't help us."

But here's what the hero's journey framework reveals: asking for help isn't the weak part of the story, it's the turning point. The hero who refuses the mentor's guidance stays trapped in their ordinary world. The hero who accepts help crosses the threshold into transformation.

Think of the last time you helped someone. The chances are high that helping made you feel good. If someone were to help you, they would likely feel good too, so why would you deny them that feeling by not asking?

Andy suggests reframing asking for help as giving people a gift; the gift of being part of your hero's journey. When you ask for guidance, you're not showing weakness; you're demonstrating the courage to grow.

The prevailing myth of the "self-made person" contradicts every hero story ever told. We grow through the help of others and only get that help when we ask. In your journey to unlock potential, asking for help isn't optional, it's the step that transforms ordinary people into heroes.

BE AN IGNITER

When you master the art of creating belief and belonging, you become an igniter of excellence in others. You become someone whose very presence makes others believe in themselves and feel they belong to something meaningful.

This shift from developing individuals to influencing movements requires a fundamentally new approach to leadership. The old command-and-control models that worked in stable, predictable environments crumble when everything changes rapidly. When AI can process information faster than any human and automate decisions that once required management oversight, what does leadership even mean?

The leaders who will shape the next decade won't be those with the best relationship with AI, though that matters. They will be the ones who remember that behind every algorithm is a human being with unlimited potential waiting to be awakened. They will understand that while machines can optimize processes, only humans can ignite the belief and belonging that transforms ordinary teams into extraordinary forces for change.

This is Leadership 4.0; not a better version of traditional leadership, but an entirely new paradigm designed for an age when human and AI must work together. It requires leaders who can navigate impossible challenges while developing human potential, just like the team that had to reimagine what it meant to create technology for the final frontier.

CHAPTER 10

LEADERSHIP 4.0

"There can be no leadership if no one follows"

— Platow, Haslam, Reicher, and Steffens

Y ou now understand the foundations of human potential in the AI age. Adversity reveals what we're capable of when tested. The Goldilocks Zone creates optimal conditions where potential can flourish. Belief and belonging provide the psychological fuel that transforms possibility into performance. But here's the crucial question: How do you systematically create these conditions for others?

Individual hero transformation is just the beginning. The leaders who will shape the next decade aren't those who've merely unlocked their own potential, they're the ones who can architect environments where human potential flourishes at scale alongside AI.

This requires an entirely new approach to leadership, one designed specifically for an age when human and artificial intelligence must work together. Welcome to Leadership 4.0.

WHEN ENGINEERS BECOME SPACE TECHNOLOGY EXPERTS

When NASA challenged HP to create a printer for the International Space Station, Anneliese Olson and her team faced an impossible puzzle. How do you make ink flow without gravity? How do you prevent paper from floating away mid-print? How do you design for an environment where every assumption about "normal" operation breaks down?

The engineers could have approached this as a technical problem, modified existing designs, added constraints, and made incremental improvements. Instead, something remarkable happened. The team began thinking like explorers rather than engineers. They didn't just solve a printing problem; they reimagined what printing could become in an entirely new context.

The banner on Olson's LinkedIn page shows a picture of her and some of her team having fun and experiencing zero gravity on NASA's "Vomit Comet" parabolic flight aircraft. The parabolic flights were to test printer prototypes in brief periods of weightlessness.

This transformation from problem-solvers to possibility-creators represents exactly what's happening to leadership in the AI age. The HP team's breakthrough came from reimagining their environment; abandoning Earth-based assumptions to succeed in space. But environmental transformation alone isn't enough. The most crucial breakthrough happens internally, when leaders develop the capacity to make value-aligned decisions regardless of external pressure. This inner development determines whether external innovation serves human flourishing or merely optimizes for narrow metrics.

THE INNER WORK OF LEADERSHIP TRANSFORMATION

Arsen Tomsky built a tech unicorn worth $1.23 billion, relocated 1,000 employees across countries during wartime, and transformed a social media portal into a global ride-hailing platform. Yet he credits none of these external achievements as his greatest leadership accomplishment.

I learned about Arsen's mindset in preparation for providing leadership development for his company, inDrive. I read his autobiography, *Inner Drive*, and we shared a meal and conversation in Almaty, Kazakhstan.

"To get into the highest level of business, an entrepreneur needs either one-in-a-million luck or move independently into the highest level of personal and spiritual growth" (Tomsky, 2024).

Notice what he's saying: external leadership success depends on internal leadership mastery. This isn't a self-help platitude; it's strategic necessity in the AI age.

Born in Yakutsk, Russia – the coldest major city in the world, where winters reach minus 50 degrees Celsius – Tomsky learned early that survival required both external adaptation and internal resilience. When he founded inDrive in 2013, he applied this same principle to business: succeed by developing your inner capabilities, not just your external strategies.

The real test came in 2022. When Russia invaded Ukraine, Tomsky faced an impossible choice: compromise his values or sacrifice his business. Traditional leadership would have focused on external factors, market analysis, stakeholder pressure, and competitive positioning.

But Tomsky had spent years developing what he calls "inner drive," the self-leadership capacity to make value-aligned decisions regardless of external pressure.

He chose to relocate his entire company. Not because it was profitable (it wasn't), not because it was easy (it certainly wasn't), but because his internal development had created the clarity and courage to act on principle.

Here's the Leadership 4.0 insight: Tomsky's business success wasn't separate from his personal development; it was the direct result of it. He used tools like the Wheel of Life assessment not as personal hobbies but as a business strategy. By continuously upgrading his self-awareness, emotional regulation, and value alignment, he built the internal capacity to lead through unprecedented external change.

This is what sets Leadership 4.0 apart from previous models. It's not about having better strategies or more advanced tools; it's about having the internal development to use any strategy or tool wisely.

Leadership 4.0 requires not just individual transformation but team evolution. When executive leadership teams function as true collaborators rather than competing silos, they model the potential-focused culture the entire organization needs.

Tomsky's inner work enabled outer impact. But what does this look like systematically? How do we move from individual transformation to organizational evolution?

WHY LEADERSHIP MUST EVOLVE NOW

The HP space printer team exemplifies Leadership 4.0 in action. When every assumption about "normal" breaks down, leaders can cling to outdated models or evolve entirely new approaches. The choice isn't optional, it's existential.

Consider what made the HP team successful:

- They embraced uncertainty as creative fuel.
- They integrated human ingenuity with cutting-edge technology.
- They distributed decision-making to the people closest to the problem.
- They maintained ethical responsibility while pushing boundaries.

These aren't just nice-to-have leadership qualities anymore. They're survival skills.

But before we can lead others through this transformation, we must first upgrade ourselves. This is where most leadership development fails and where one CEO's journey offers a powerful blueprint.

THE PSYCHOLOGY OF LEADERSHIP 4.0

Christopher M. Barlow, PhD, teaches his MBA students a counterintuitive truth: "There is no such thing as a person having leadership." Instead, people have a process of follower-ship, trusting certain people on specific issues. When someone invokes that followership response, we call it leadership.

This distinction matters enormously in the AI age. Traditional leadership (1.0 through 3.0) relied on position, information, or expertise advantages. But when AI can access more information and analyze it faster than any human, what creates followership?

The answer brings us back to the HP space printer team. People followed their lead not because of their technical knowledge but because of their human qualities: curiosity about impossible problems, courage to reimagine solutions, and care for the larger mission.

Leadership 4.0 influence emerges from human capabilities that AI cannot replicate.

WHAT IS LEADERSHIP 4.0?

Leadership 4.0 is the systematic orchestration of human potential and AI to create unprecedented value while preserving what makes us irreplaceably human. Unlike previous leadership models that focused on managing people or processes, Leadership 4.0 architects environments where human creativity, wisdom, and connection amplify AI capabilities, while AI handles routine cognitive work that frees humans for higher-order thinking, relationship building, and moral reasoning. See Figure 10.1.

Core Distinction: Previous leadership models assumed human limitations and designed systems around those constraints. Leadership 4.0 assumes human potential is unlimited when properly supported by AI, and designs systems to continuously expand what humans can achieve.

The Evolution of Leadership

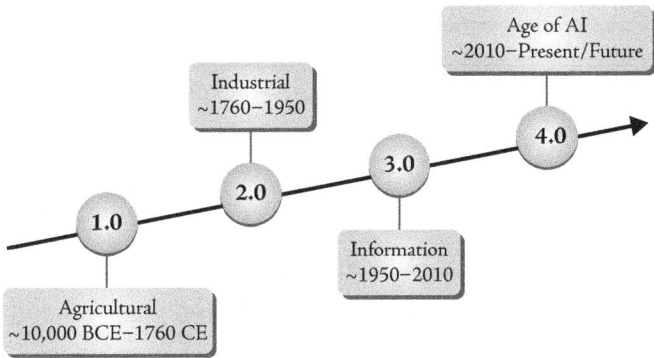

Figure 10.1   The Evolution of Leadership

Leadership 4.0 doesn't replace human judgment with AI—
it amplifies human judgment through intelligent partnership.

THE FOUR DYNAMICS OF LEADERSHIP 4.0

Just as the HP space printer required four interconnected
systems that worked together dynamically (pressure regulation, paper handling, safety systems, and compact design),
Leadership 4.0 operates through four fluid, evolving dynamics. Unlike static pillars that stand separately, these dynamics flow into and amplify each other, creating an adaptive
leadership system designed for continuous evolution.

DYNAMIC 1: HUMAN-AI SYMBIOSIS → FROM REPLACEMENT TO AMPLIFICATION

This is not just about using AI; it's about redesigning how
intelligence itself operates in your organization. Leaders

orchestrate ecosystems where human wisdom and artificial processing power create capabilities neither could
achieve alone.

Microsoft's Evolution: When Satya Nadella transformed
Microsoft, he didn't just add AI features to existing products.
He reimagined the company as a learning organism where AI
augments human decision-making at every level. Engineers
spend less time debugging code (AI handles that) and more
time solving complex human problems. Sales teams use AI for
data analysis while focusing their human energy on relationship building and creative solution design. The result: company valuation grew from $300 billion to $3 trillion because
human potential expanded rather than being replaced.

The Dynamic in Practice: Leadership 4.0 leaders continuously ask: "How can AI amplify what makes us most
human?" They design workflows where machines handle
pattern recognition while humans provide context, creativity, and moral judgment. This dynamic evolves as AI capabilities expand. What required human intelligence yesterday
becomes automated today, freeing humans for higher-order
thinking tomorrow.

DYNAMIC 2: DISTRIBUTED INTELLIGENCE → FROM HIERARCHY TO NETWORK

Decision-making flows to wherever the optimal combination of human insight, AI capability, and contextual knowledge intersects, regardless of organizational chart positions.
Leaders become intelligence architects, designing systems
where good decisions emerge from the network rather than
cascade from the top.

Haier's Transformation: Zhang Ruimin didn't just flatten hierarchy by removing middle managers; he created 4,000 self-organizing teams, each equipped with real-time AI analytics and direct customer feedback loops. Teams make pricing, product development, and partnership decisions at market speed because they have both the information (AI-powered) and authority (human-granted) to act. Revenue jumped from $4.8 billion to $35 billion because intelligence became distributed throughout the organization, not bottlenecked at the top.

The Dynamic in Practice: This requires leaders who can tolerate apparent chaos while designing underlying systems for coherent action. They create clear principles and boundaries, then trust distributed teams to make smart decisions within those parameters. As AI provides better real-time information, decision-making can be pushed even further to the edges where customer problems actually exist.

DYNAMIC 3: LEARNING VELOCITY → FROM KNOWING TO BECOMING

Organizations transform into continuous-learning laboratories where people don't just adapt to change; they architect it. Every role becomes an experiment in human potential development, with AI accelerating the feedback loops that enable rapid capability evolution.

Google's Reinvention: Sundar Pichai's "AI-first" strategy required every employee to reimagine their relationship to their work. Software engineers learned to collaborate with AI coding partners. Marketers learned to interpret AI-generated consumer insights. Customer service teams learned to use AI for routine queries while developing deeper empathy skills for complex human problems. The company didn't just train people on new tools; they redesigned jobs to assume continuous evolution alongside AI advancement.

The Dynamic in Practice: Leaders measure learning velocity alongside traditional performance metrics. They ask: "How quickly do our people absorb new capabilities?" and "How effectively do they apply new learning to novel situations?" This dynamic accelerates as AI handles more routine tasks, creating space for humans to focus on capability development that machines can't replicate.

DYNAMIC 4: ETHICAL EVOLUTION → FROM COMPLIANCE TO MORAL ARCHITECTURE

Every AI implementation becomes an opportunity to encode human values at scale. Leaders become moral architects, designing systems that don't just optimize for efficiency but actively promote human flourishing and societal benefit.

Salesforce's Approach: Marc Benioff created the Office of Ethical and Humane Use of Technology not as a compliance afterthought but as a core business function. Every AI feature undergoes ethical review alongside technical testing. When developing Einstein AI, teams built bias detection directly into the algorithm's architecture, not as an external check. Customer trust became a competitive advantage because ethical consideration was embedded in product development from day one.

The Dynamic in Practice: This requires leaders who can hold both short-term business pressures and long-term human consequences in creative tension. They ask not just "Can we do this?" but "Should we do this?" and "What kind of world are we creating?" As AI capabilities expand, these ethical decisions become more complex and more crucial to sustainable success.

THE INTERCONNECTED FLOW

These dynamics don't operate in sequence; they flow into and amplify each other continuously.

Symbiosis Enables Distribution: When humans and AI work seamlessly together, decision-making can be safely distributed because both human wisdom and AI are available at every node.

Distribution Accelerates Learning: When decision-making is distributed, learning happens faster because feedback loops are shorter and experiments can run in parallel across the organization.

Learning Informs Ethics: Rapid learning reveals unintended consequences faster, enabling ethical course corrections before problems scale.

Ethics Guides Symbiosis: Clear values help determine which human–AI partnerships serve human flourishing and which merely optimize for narrow metrics.

The Complete System in Action: The outdoor apparel and gear company, Patagonia demonstrates all four dynamics simultaneously. Their human–AI symbiosis uses technology to serve environmental activism (values-driven). Their distributed intelligence allows any employee to propose environmental initiatives regardless of hierarchy position. Their learning velocity helps teams rapidly adapt to new environmental challenges and opportunities. Their ethical evolution ensures every business decision gets filtered through environmental impact considerations.

EVOLUTION, NOT DESTINATION

Leadership 4.0 isn't a final form; it's an adaptive system designed to evolve alongside technological and social change. As AI capabilities expand, these dynamics will deepen and new dynamics may emerge. The leaders who thrive will be those who master not just these four dynamics, but the meta-skill of evolving their leadership approach as the context continues to change.

This is why traditional leadership development fails in the AI age: it treats leadership as a fixed set of skills rather than an evolving set of dynamics. Leadership 4.0 leaders don't just learn new capabilities; they continuously redesign how capability development happens in the first place.

The HP space printer team succeeded because they intuitively understood these dynamics: they combined human creativity with AI modeling (symbiosis), distributed problem-solving to whoever had the best ideas (distributed intelligence), learned zero-gravity physics while working (learning velocity), and kept every decision aligned with the mission of space exploration (ethical evolution).

Your challenge isn't to master these four dynamics at once, but to continuously evolve your mastery as the AI revolution unfolds. The question isn't whether you'll change, but whether you'll architect that change intentionally or let it happen to you.

LEADERSHIP 4.0 IN ACTION: THE COMPLETE IGNITE SYSTEM

The IGNITE framework enables systematic Leadership 4.0 implementation. The connection between the four dynamics and the IGNITE framework can be seen here:

- Symbiosis enables INTEGRATE
- Distributed intelligence powers GUIDE
- Learning velocity drives TRANSFORM
- Ethical evolution anchors INSPIRE

Leaders create the culture of the organization by the way they nurture their people, and smart leaders constantly evaluate what is working and what can be improved.

Patagonia's evolution from an outdoor gear company to an environmental movement provides an excellent case study to look at the execution of the IGNITE framework.

Inspire Through Purpose: Vincent Stanley, Patagonia's Director of Philosophy, created the counter-consumerism "Don't Buy This Jacket" campaign. In 2011, while marketing teams across America were running Black Friday sales campaigns, Patagonia published a full-page ad in *The New York Times* featuring its best-selling jacket with the headline, "Don't Buy This Jacket": telling customers not to purchase their products unless necessary. This counterintuitive approach revealed something profound: authentic purpose unlocks potential in both employees and customers.

Guide Through Questions: Instead of micromanaging environmental initiatives, leaders ask: "What environmental issue keeps you awake at night?" This shifts people from order-followers to solution-creators.

When employee Ryan Gellert (now CEO) proposed aggressive carbon-neutrality goals that seemed impossible, Patagonia's founder, Yvon Chouinard, responded:

"That sounds exactly like the kind of challenge that will force us to innovate. What support do you need to make it happen?"

Chouinard's response to Gellert illustrates a crucial Leadership 4.0 principle: instead of managing people toward predetermined outcomes, leaders guide them toward discovering their own extraordinary capabilities.

Nurture Belief and Belonging: Employees aren't just gear company workers; they are environmental activists who happen to work for Patagonia. This identity transformation unleashes capabilities people didn't know they had.

Patagonia built an Ubuntu-style culture of belonging. Instead of being onboarded as "outdoor gear company employees," new hires are welcomed as "environmental activists who happen to work for Patagonia."

Patagonia's philosophy demonstrates how Leadership 4.0 creates what we might call "potential contagion." This is beyond traditional employee development. Leadership 4.0 creates environments where people's potential becomes visible to themselves and everyone around them.

INTEGRATE AI Tools Strategically: Patagonia does something smart with AI; they make it serve their bigger purpose instead of the other way around. Before implementing any new technology, they ask: "Does this help the planet or at least not hurt it?" It's a simple filter that keeps them honest about why they're in business.

"Philosophy eats AI" is an insightful article published in the *MIT Sloan Management Review* (Schrage, 2025). Authors Michael Shrage and David Kiron argue that generating sustainable business value with AI demands critical thinking about the disparate philosophies determining AI development, training, deployment, and use. Patagonia is already doing this.

Their Worn Wear program is a prime example. AI observes customer usage patterns, product longevity, and repair needs. Patagonia employees interpret what these patterns mean for environmental impact and customer relationships. AI recommends personalized repair guides and sustainable usage tips, and humans ignite customers to see gear maintenance as environmental activism.

TRANSFORM Through Challenge and Support: Former CEO Rose Marcario is a case study for the challenge and support approach. When Marcario joined Patagonia in 2008, she was a high-performing finance executive comfortable with financial metrics and operational efficiency, but Chouinard saw something beyond this.

Marcario was first challenged to integrate environmental impact metrics into all financial reporting. Once this was successfully completed, the challenge was escalated to lead Patagonia's environmental finance integration. This meant deciding which grassroots organizations should receive funding.

Marcario's breakthrough moment came after she recommended funding organizations fighting dam removal.

"Seeing those rivers run free because of decisions I helped make, that's when I understood the power of business as environmental activism. I wasn't just moving money around; I was helping restore ecosystems."

This wasn't just a career change; it was potential realization. Her identity had transformed from "I'm a finance person" to "I'm an environmental strategist who uses financial tools."

The complete IGNITE system works because it addresses both individual development and organizational transformation. However, implementing it requires leaders who can assess their own readiness for this evolution.

Understanding how the four dynamics work together is just the beginning. The real transformation happens when leaders start implementing these principles systematically. Here is a roadmap to activate Leadership 4.0 in your organization.

LEADERSHIP 4.0 TRANSFORMATION ROADMAP

"In the age of AI, your ability to learn continuously is your only sustainable competitive advantage"

– Sundar Pichai, 2019

Leadership 4.0 isn't implemented overnight; it's cultivated through systematic progression. Like the HP space printer team, you need to test, learn, and iterate. Here's your 90-day roadmap to begin the transformation.

PHASE 1: FOUNDATION (DAYS 1–30) – START WITH YOURSELF

Before you can architect human potential in others, you must develop your own Leadership 4.0 capacity. Use the IGNITE framework as your personal development system.

Weeks 1 and 2: Self-Assessment

- **INSPIRE Check:** What's your authentic purpose beyond profit? Write one sentence.
- **GUIDE Assessment:** Who are your mentors for navigating AI transformation? If none, identify three potential guides.
- **NURTURE Review:** Do you feel psychologically safe to experiment and fail? If not, what needs to change?

Weeks 3 and 4: Personal AI Partnership

- Choose one routine task and experiment with AI assistance (ChatGPT, Claude, Copilot).
- Track: What human capabilities were freed up? How did you use that time?
- Reflect: What uniquely human value did you add that AI couldn't?

PHASE 2: TEAM EXPERIMENTATION (DAYS 31–60) – CREATE SMALL WINS

Dynamic 1 Pilot: Human–AI Symbiosis

- Select your most routine team process (reporting, analysis, scheduling).
- Introduce AI assistance while requiring human interpretation and decision-making.
- Measure: Time saved + quality of human insights generated.
- Example: Use AI to analyze customer feedback data while humans focus on creative solutions.

Dynamic 2 Test: Distributed Intelligence

- Identify one decision currently requiring your approval.
- Create clear criteria and boundaries, then delegate to whoever has best context + AI access.
- Document: Decision quality, speed, team confidence.
- Debrief: What would you do differently? What surprised you?

PHASE 3: SYSTEMATIC INTEGRATION (DAYS 61–90) – SCALE WHAT WORKS

IGNITE Your Team Culture

- **INSPIRE:** Share your Learning 4.0 purpose story. Ask: "What impossible problem could we solve together?"
- **GUIDE:** Replace one weekly status meeting with a "What did AI help you discover this week?" session.
- **NURTURE:** Create "intelligent failure" celebrations, when human–AI experiments don't work as expected.

- **INTEGRATE:** Establish team protocols for when to use AI versus human judgment.
- **TRANSFORM:** Give everyone a "stretch assignment" requiring both AI assistance and human creativity.
- **EVALUATE:** Monthly team reflection: "Are we becoming more human or more robotic?"

SUCCESS INDICATORS AT 90 DAYS

Individual Transformation

- You regularly use AI as a thinking partner, not just a tool.
- You can clearly articulate what makes your leadership irreplaceably human.
- You're comfortable making decisions with incomplete information but clear values.

Team Evolution

- Team members proactively suggest human–AI collaboration improvements.
- Decision-making speed increased without sacrificing quality.
- People feel more energized by their work, not depleted by it.

Organizational Signs

- Other teams are asking, "How can we work like that?"
- Customer/stakeholder feedback mentions increased innovation or responsiveness.
- You're attracting talent that wants to grow, not just earn.

COMMON OBSTACLES AND SOLUTIONS

"My team resists AI tools"

- Start with AI helping them do current work better, not replacing their work.
- Share specific examples of how AI freed you up for more meaningful activities.
- Let early adopters become peer teachers rather than mandating from above.

"Our culture isn't ready for distributed decision-making"

- Begin with reversible decisions and clear escalation criteria.
- Celebrate when distributed decisions work well.
- Share the business case: speed and quality improve when decision-makers have both context and authority.

"I don't have time for this transformation"

- Leadership 4.0 isn't additional work; it's a different way of working.
- Start with 15 minutes daily of AI-assisted reflection on your leadership.
- Ask: "What would I stop doing if AI could handle the routine parts of this?"

BEYOND 90 DAYS: CONTINUOUS EVOLUTION

Leadership 4.0 is an adaptive system, not a destination. As AI capabilities expand, your leadership must evolve. Schedule quarterly reviews.

- What new AI capabilities can amplify human potential?
- Which human capabilities are becoming more valuable as AI advances?
- How is our culture evolving to support human–AI collaboration?
- What ethical boundaries need updating as technology advances?

YOUR LEADERSHIP 4.0 JOURNEY STARTS NOW

The HP space printer team succeeded because they understood a fundamental truth: you can't succeed with minor modifications when the environment changes completely. You need a complete reimagining.

Leadership 4.0 isn't Leadership 3.0 with AI tools added. It fundamentally reimagines what leadership means when human and AI work together. It requires leaders who can develop themselves as intensely as Arsen Tomsky, inspire teams as effectively as the HP engineers, and create movements as powerful as Patagonia's environmental transformation.

The question isn't whether this evolution will happen, it's whether you'll lead it or be left behind.

Your choice is simple but not easy

- Continue leading with industrial-age models while AI transforms everything around you.
- Or become a Leadership 4.0 architect who unlocks human potential at scale.

The foundations are in your hands. You understand how adversity reveals capability, how to create Goldilocks Zones where potential flourishes, and how belief and belonging fuel transformation. You have the IGNITE framework and the four dynamics. You have examples of leaders who've made this transition successfully.

What you do next will determine not just your leadership legacy, but the kind of future your organization creates in the intelligence age.

The printer is waiting. The space station needs what only you can provide. Your team's potential is calling.

Will you answer?

CHAPTER 11

HIRE FOR TOMORROW, NOT YESTERDAY

Chapter 10 introduced Leadership 4.0: the systematic orchestration of human potential and AI. You have the IGNITE framework and a 90-day roadmap to implement it.

But here's the uncomfortable truth: you can't build a Leadership 4.0 organization with industrial-age hiring practices.

Every job description written for yesterday's challenges, every interview focused on past experience rather than future potential, every hiring decision that prioritizes rigid qualifications over learning velocity actively undermines everything you're trying to create.

The HP space printer team didn't succeed because they had zero-gravity experience. Patagonia's environmental movement didn't emerge from hiring people with "environmental activism" on their resumes. Each breakthrough happened because someone saw potential where others saw missing checkboxes on an application form.

If you're serious about Leadership 4.0, you must completely reimagine how you find, assess, and develop people. The leaders who will thrive in the intelligence age aren't sitting in your talent pipeline. They're being overlooked by hiring processes designed for a world that no longer exists.

The Tetris Trap: Why We're Hiring for Yesterday's Game

Your organization's future depends on the people you haven't yet hired. But if you're still recruiting like it's 1995, you're assembling a team for yesterday's challenges while tomorrow's opportunities slip away.

Herdis Pala Palsdottir, a global Human Resources (HR) expert from Iceland, has watched this tragedy unfold for decades. She has seen talented people get overlooked, not because they lacked potential, but because they didn't fit the shape of predetermined boxes.

"We are always hiring people to fit in some boxes," she explains, her voice carrying the frustration of an HR professional who has seen this pattern repeat countless times. "It's like a Tetris game. You only have a few open Tetris spaces, and people can't always fit in – or don't want to squeeze themselves into those boxes, not having their expectations or needs met."

The metaphor is perfect, and you can't unsee it once you see it. In Tetris, success depends on fitting predetermined shapes into predetermined spaces. The pieces fall from the sky in fixed configurations, straight lines, L-shapes, squares, and Z-shapes. Your job isn't to reimagine the pieces but to find where they fit in the existing structure.

Traditional hiring works the same way. Organizations create job descriptions like Tetris pieces, which are fixed shapes with rigid requirements. "Must have five years of experience in X." "Requires certification in Y." "Degree in Z preferred." Then they wait for candidates who match those exact specifications to fall from the sky.

But here's what Tetris doesn't teach you about human potential: people aren't geometric shapes. They're more like water – adaptable, capable of taking the form of whatever container holds them and finding paths around obstacles that would stop a rigid block.

What if. . .

What if instead of asking. . .	We asked. . .
"Do you fit this job?"	"What could you build here?"
"Have you done this before?"	"How quickly can you figure this out?"
"Do you match our requirements?"	"What would be possible if we designed something around your unique capabilities?"

The Tetris approach works fine when the game stays the same. But what happens when the rules change completely? When AI can handle pattern recognition, data analysis, and routine decision-making, suddenly your perfectly fitted "pieces" become liabilities. The rigid shapes that once seemed so valuable now can't adapt to an entirely new playing field.

Smart organizations are realizing they need to stop playing Tetris altogether and hire people with learning velocity. They're recognizing that in the AI age, people strategy and technology strategy aren't separate games with separate rules. They're the same game, requiring integrated thinking from the very top.

That's exactly what Moderna discovered when they made a decision that shocked the corporate world.

THE MODERNA REVOLUTION

While most companies debate whether to hire Chief AI Officers or upgrade their HR technology, Moderna, the vaccine maker, decided to defy conventional wisdom. In 2024, they merged two of their most critical leadership roles: Chief People Officer and Chief Digital Officer, into a single position.

This wasn't cost-cutting or organizational streamlining. This was recognition of a fundamental truth that most companies are still avoiding. In the age of AI, you cannot build people strategies without considering technology, and you cannot implement technology without understanding human impact.

Moderna's bold move reflects what *The Wall Street Journal* called "rethinking workforce planning due to the growing capabilities of AI" (Bousquette, 2025). Instead of treating HR and AI as separate domains, they acknowledged what 4.0 leaders already know: the future belongs to organizations that can orchestrate human–AI collaboration from the ground up.

This integration challenges every assumption about traditional hiring. When your Chief People Officer is also your Chief Digital Officer, job descriptions become capability maps, performance reviews become potential assessments, and hiring decisions become strategic bets on human–AI partnerships rather than individual qualifications.

Moderna's approach embodies the INTEGRATE element of the IGNITE framework. They're not just using AI tools in HR but reimagining human development through the lens of technological possibility.

This integration signals a fundamental shift across industries: from viewing people and technology as separate challenges to recognizing them as inseparable strategic elements.

Learning Velocity Revolution

Steve Cadigan has witnessed the evolution of hiring from inside Silicon Valley's most successful companies. As LinkedIn's first Chief HR Officer, he's seen what works, what doesn't, and what's coming next. His prediction about the future of hiring isn't just theory, it's an inevitable shift that forward-thinking companies are already implementing.

"Most people I talk to think we have a recruiting problem right now," Steve observes. "And I'm saying no, we don't.

We have a skill awareness problem tied to potential and understanding raw talent over experience."

The traditional hiring playbook is becoming obsolete. For decades, companies have hired for what they needed yesterday, not what they'll need tomorrow. Job descriptions get "mimeographed, then xeroxed," outdated requirements copied and pasted without thought. Recruiters focus on experience, credentials, and past performance in similar roles.

But Steve sees a fundamental shift coming: "We're gonna see more people hired on what they can learn than on what they know."

This isn't wishful thinking, it's survival. "If you believe, like I do, that jobs are changing faster, markets are changing faster, the need for new skills has never been greater, I need people to learn new stuff quickly. I need to hire for learning velocity."

"I need to know that you can learn stuff quickly, and you're a self-study. You've got a growth mindset. You're a curious person, and I need to know that when the job changes, you're changing or you're changing the job."

Steve predicts we'll start seeing CVs and LinkedIn profiles showcasing learning agility rather than job titles.

This doesn't mean experience becomes worthless. It means that rigid experience becomes a liability while adaptive experience becomes an asset. The question shifts from "How long have you been doing this?" to "How effectively do you learn when everything changes?"

For candidates, this means building a portfolio of learning rather than just a portfolio of achievements. It means demonstrating intellectual agility, not just domain expertise. It means showing evidence of growing through challenges, not just succeeding in familiar environments.

For organizations, it means developing new ways to assess potential that goes beyond resume screening. It means looking for a growth mindset, curiosity, and resilience rather than just technical qualifications. It means designing roles that assume change rather than roles that assume stability.

The learning velocity revolution isn't coming, it's already here. The question isn't whether this shift will happen, but whether your organization will be ahead or behind.

PREPARING THE BRAVE GENERATION

"Success, for me, is doing what you like, with people you enjoy"
– Tim Viera

I was recently in Sri Lanka, preparing to speak about self-leadership and its potential for empowering a nation. I caught up with a previous client, Chathuranga Abeysinghe, who is now the Deputy Minister for Industrial and Entrepreneurship Development.

We discussed many of Sri Lanka's challenges, and he made a very strong point: "Organizations must partner with schools and universities to inform them of the skills they will need."

If schools and universities are still turning out cogs for a machine that no longer exists, we are going to be in real trouble.

We need a more agile education system, and it does exist – in pockets.

I visited a Brave Generation Academy (BGA) hub in Cascais, 30 minutes from where I live in Portugal. The BGA is the brainchild of entrepreneur Tim Vieira. Tim was born in South Africa, the son of a Portuguese father and a Mozambican mother, both teachers. Tim established the BGA in 2020 when he realized there was a problem in education. Many children don't succeed in traditional schools because they don't fit in with the current educational system, which lacks personalization and fails to recognize individual differences. Tim told me that as an entrepreneur, he found many young people possessed certificates but lacked the skills that a modern workplace demands.

Instead of traditional teachers, students work with learning coaches who develop self-directed learning capabilities. Students master academic content while building the autonomy and technological fluency that integrated organizations require.

When Moderna's leadership decided that people strategy and technology strategy were inseparable, they were betting on graduates from this kind of educational philosophy: learners who see AI as amplification, not replacement.

This educational revolution reveals what Moderna and other progressive organizations understand: the most valuable skills can't be taught through traditional methods or assessed through conventional interviews.

This educational revolution is already influencing how progressive leaders think about talent development.

But what does this mean for organizations hiring today? How do you identify candidates who embody this new learning philosophy when most still come from traditional educational backgrounds?

THE NEW HIRING FRAMEWORK

Manish Bundhun was once a student in one of my programs, and today, he is the Chief People Officer at the ENL Group. His role spans eight industries across twelve countries and oversees HR for approximately 7,500 employees. He describes himself as "The Corporate Monk," bringing mindfulness, presence, and wisdom to the corporate environment. Manish and I agreed that we need to upgrade: "As artificial intelligence increases, we as human beings need to augment our intelligence to match artificial intelligence."

Manish believes humans must develop multiple forms of emotional, social, and spiritual intelligence to remain relevant despite AI advancements.

Unfortunately, most organizations impose Sparta-like constraints that prevent people from maximizing their potential through rigid structures, competency frameworks, and limited psychological safety. The core problem is an archaic view of employees as economic units of production rather than potential that can be unleashed.

With such a broad portfolio, I asked Manish, "Is your human resource work the same across industries and sectors, or do they have different challenges?"

He replied that 80% of the challenges were the same: how do you attract, develop, and retain talent?

Manish identifies three crucial Leadership 4.0 qualities:

- The ability to spot potential in people.
- The ability to nurture and grow that potential.
- The willingness to continuously upskill oneself.

He emphasizes that organizations too often uproot underperforming talent rather than improving the conditions for their flourishing.

Manish distinguishes between managers and leaders in their hiring approaches:

- Managers ask HR: "Hire me someone who can fill the job"
- 4.0 leaders ask HR: "Let's hire talent that can grow with us"

Manish's distinction between managers who "hire someone to fill the job" and leaders who "hire talent that can grow with us" raises a crucial question: How do you actually assess growth potential in an interview? The answer requires upgrading our most fundamental interview techniques.

FINDING 4.0 STARS

The good news is that we don't have to throw out our interview skills, but we do have to upgrade them if we want to find people for a Leadership 4.0 environment.

You've probably been through STAR interviews, those "Tell me about a time when. . ." questions. They've been around since the 1970s, and they work pretty well for understanding what someone has done. But they don't tell you much about how they think, which is what really matters now.

The original STAR framework consists of four key elements.

1. **Situation:** Setting the scene by describing the context or circumstances faced.
2. **Task:** Explaining the specific responsibility or goal in that situation.
3. **Action:** Detailing the specific steps taken to address the situation.
4. **Result:** Sharing the outcomes achieved through actions, ideally with measurable impacts.

The framework can be used to elicit past behaviors as predictors of future performance or to showcase the candidate's past experiences.

Manish Bundhun upgraded the STAR interview technique to replace "Task" with "Thinking" when interviewing talent.

For example. "What was your thinking at that moment? What action did you take, and what was the result?"

Asking, "What was your thinking?" reveals cognitive patterns that predict potential. But what if we could analyze these patterns at scale, detecting subtle indicators that even experienced interviewers might miss? This is where AI transforms from threat to opportunity.

AI INTERVIEWS

Interviewing is arguably one of the areas where AI can do a better job than humans, but only if we use it to amplify human insight rather than replace human judgment. Well-designed AI systems can minimize unconscious biases that commonly affect human judgment (similarity bias, halo effect, and confirmation bias). AI can be programmed to ignore demographic factors and focus solely on qualifications and responses relevant to the job. AI can analyze patterns across thousands of interviews to identify predictors of success that humans might miss. AI systems can detect subtle linguistic patterns, micro-expressions, and problem-solving approaches that correlate with future job performance.

But there's a predictable trap to avoid: using AI to optimize for yesterday's hiring criteria instead of tomorrow's potential. This will find perfect matches for outdated job descriptions rather than identifying people who can grow, adapt, and thrive alongside AI.

Imagine instead a **self-leadership assessment** that analyzes speech patterns, response consistency, and decision-making frameworks to identify candidates who demonstrate agency and self-direction. For example, AI might detect when candidates take ownership ("I decided to. . .") versus showing victim mentality ("They made me. . ."). The system could identify patterns that indicate an internal locus of control, the foundation of self-leadership.

AI can detect **learning velocity**. It can analyze thousands of responses to identify linguistic markers that indicate rapid learning ability. It looks for evidence of curiosity, growth mindset, and intellectual humility, the markers Steve Cadigan identified as crucial for the future workforce.

Candidates will be asked to describe how they approached learning something completely new. AI can then analyze their learning strategy, adaptability indicators, and metacognitive awareness (thinking about thinking).

AI can assess how naturally candidates think about **human–technology collaboration**. It can spot those who see AI as amplification rather than threat, who instinctively think in terms of symbiosis rather than replacement.

Example Scenario: "You're given access to an AI tool that can analyze customer data faster than any human. How would you use it to improve customer relationships?"

AI evaluates whether responses show symbiosis thinking (using AI insights to enable deeper human connection) or replacement thinking (letting AI handle customer relationships entirely).

THE HUMAN + AI INTERVIEW PROCESS

The most effective approach combines AI assessment with human insight using what James Taylor calls the "centaur" model; AI handles pattern recognition while humans provide context and final judgment.

Remember: AI interviews are only as good as the human wisdom that guides them. Use technology to identify potential, but rely on human judgment to understand how that potential could flourish in your unique environment.

The future belongs to organizations that use AI to find people who can dance with uncertainty, learn at the speed of change, and maintain their humanity while amplifying their capabilities through intelligent partnership.

HIRE FOR DRIVE AND LET THEM LEARN THE REST

In a recent conversation with global futurist Rohit Talwar, we discussed a point that so many leaders overlook: "Organizational potential is a function of the extent to which you are unleashing the potential of your people."

Leadership 4.0 organizations need employees who are strong across all six dimensions of our Potential Proprioception framework.

- **Self-Leadership Awareness:** Can they maintain agency when AI handles routine tasks?
- **Competence Intelligence:** How do they approach skill gaps in rapidly changing environments?
- **Somatic Awareness:** Do they understand the human elements that AI cannot replicate?
- **Relational Intelligence:** How effectively do they collaborate with both humans and AI systems?
- **Purpose Alignment:** Can they maintain meaning when technology automates their previous role?

- **Integration Capacity:** How naturally do they combine human insight with AI?"

I previously introduced you to Anneliese Olson, the President of HP's Imaging, Printing, and Solutions. She told me, "To turn strategy into reality, you only do that through and with people. You could be selling diapers or making airplanes; business is human, and people are the center of that. Because of my background in sports, I could see very visually how important it is to unlock potential in others. And then the ripple effect that you have in terms of, you know, having broader and broader scopes or responsibility for teams where, you know, it's not just this one-on-one relationship and all the things that you do, but how do you, create that space and get alignment and ideally unlock the best in other people, all around the world, even when you're not in the room."

Anneliese is a people-oriented 4.0 leader who acknowledges that this evolved over time, but she credits her mindset to her early college basketball experience. "Whether it was playing basketball and having peers and colleagues that I was working with and the role that I knew that I needed to play on a team or being in the C-Suite now and understanding here's my business, what do I need to get done with, with and through people."

I asked Anneliesse about identifying potential.

"You think about what signals indicate what people could be doing, not just past performances. How scalable are people? How agile are they? Is there a growth mindset and a desire for learning?"

As we have discussed before, learning is the catalyst to potentialize. When you learn, you expand your aperture regarding what you can take in and the connections you can make.

An organization like HP looks at how a person might scale over the next two, five, and ten years. They look for the signals we previously discussed, such as self-efficacy, curiosity, and problem-solving, and the ability to take feedback without taking it personally.

If you are a manager or a leader, it is critical that you meet people deep within your organization and encourage them to present their work and ideas rather than just relying on your direct reports; only then will you be able to spot potential.

If your organization has a problem to solve, a good strategy for identifying potential is to form a small team of individuals with technical skills but without seniority and say, "OK, examine this problem and report back with possible solutions in two weeks." You will likely be surprised by what transpires.

HP's focus on "what people could be doing, not just past performances" reveals something crucial: the most scalable people are those who can adapt and grow. But in the AI age, the ultimate test of adaptability isn't just learning new skills – it's learning to collaborate with AI itself.

COLLABORATING WITH AI

I spoke with James Taylor, an AI and creativity speaker, about what the new world of work will look like as we collaborate with AI. His insights reveal both the immense potential and the very human obstacles we must overcome.

"For 70% of organizations that start to use AI, the initiatives get stuck in the pilot phase," James observes. "When they investigate why that's happening, they find it's because they never really add value to the organization's customers, clients, or employees."

The problem isn't technical, it's psychological. "Everyone immediately jumps into the tech piece. But you have to pause and look at what's going on in the minds of the people in the organization and why it's not working."

James identifies two primary mental barriers that prevent effective human–AI collaboration.

1. **Inertia:** "They're like – I'll get round to it." This isn't laziness; it's the natural human resistance to changing established workflows. People have invested years mastering current processes, and AI collaboration requires rebuilding those competencies from scratch.

2. **Fear:** "They're scared that it will take their jobs or their roles, or reduce their salary." This fear creates a self-defeating cycle: people avoid learning AI collaboration, which makes them more vulnerable to replacement rather than less.

James Taylor has adapted the analogy of cyborgs and centaurs to illustrate the different approaches to collaborating with AI.

The Cyborg Approach: These individuals feel completely comfortable with technology and constantly intertwine everything that they do with AI. They are like the guitar player whose instrument is an extension of who they are. Voice commands are often their preferred way to collaborate, and they use AI as a thinking partner, life coach, and capability amplifier.

Example: A marketing executive who begins every strategy session by asking AI to analyze market trends, then uses those insights to spark creative discussions with her human team. The AI handles data processing; she provides strategic interpretation and team inspiration.

The Centaur Approach: These individuals look at a project and consciously decide which tasks humans will handle and which AI will manage, then they integrate the results. They maintain clear boundaries between human and AI responsibilities while orchestrating both toward shared objectives.

Example: A product manager who uses AI to generate multiple design variations, then brings human designers together to evaluate emotional impact, brand alignment, and user experience. AI provides options; humans provide judgment.

BEYOND INDIVIDUAL COLLABORATION: TEAM INTELLIGENCE

The real breakthrough comes when entire teams learn to collaborate with AI collectively. James points out that "ideas with execution are useless. This is where AI can facilitate a super collaboration by identifying who has the right personality and skill sets to bring an idea to fruition."

What to Look for When Hiring for AI Collaboration

When you're hiring for this future, you need to identify people who can navigate the very real challenges that derail most human–AI collaborations.

THE LEADERSHIP 4.0 COLLABORATION ASSESSMENT

Collaborative Confidence: Look for candidates who are secure enough in their abilities to let AI handle what it does best while focusing on uniquely human contributions. They don't see AI capability as a threat to their identity.

Interview question: "Tell me about a time when you worked with someone who was better than you at something important. How did you handle that dynamic?"

Integration Thinking: They naturally consider both human and AI contributions when approaching problems. When presented with a challenge, they instinctively think about partnership rather than competition.

Interview question: "If you had an AI assistant that could do any analytical work instantly, what would you focus your human energy on?"

Dynamic Adaptation: They can switch fluidly between cyborg and centaur modes depending on what the situation requires. Sometimes they want AI deeply integrated; other times they prefer clear separation of roles.

Interview question: "Describe a project where you had to figure out who should do what. How did you make those decisions?"

Common Collaboration Red Flags

The Control Freak: Wants to micromanage AI outputs instead of providing strategic direction. These candidates create bottlenecks in human–AI workflows.

The Abdicator: Wants to hand everything over to AI without maintaining human oversight. These candidates miss nuances that require human judgment.

The Perfectionist: Gets stuck trying to make AI outputs perfect instead of using them as starting points for human creativity.

The Isolationist: Prefers working with AI alone rather than integrating insights into team collaboration. These candidates limit collective intelligence potential.

The future belongs to teams that can dance together – humans and AI – creating solutions that neither could achieve alone. When you're hiring, look for people who get excited about what becomes possible when human creativity combines with AI processing power.

RAISING 4.0 LEADERS

As previously mentioned, we cannot afford a leadership vacuum at this pivotal time.

Consulting firms and Chief HR Officers spend time clarifying leadership expectations and quantifying what a leader is expected to do. The problem is that the traditional approach still promotes leaders who are clones of the incumbent leaders.

Anupama Lal, Head of Learning and Culture, KPMG in Asia Pacific told me, "The hope is that organizations can create a balance where people feel comfortable putting themselves forward without fear of judgment, and where leaders who are accustomed to a traditionalist approach are open to these conversations. Creating a culture of open dialogue is key to enable potential-related conversations. This culture of dialogue is a positive shift, as it creates an environment that encourages the examination of potential rather than just past performance."

Anupama continued, "There is always more to do with the changing times and the culture transformation all organizations need to facilitate. It is important to keep focus and continue to make the shifts we want to see happen. We can all do a lot more work on cultural intelligence, managing biases, and creating spaces for people to learn how to engage in reflective practices."

The Tetris game is ending, but the alternative isn't chaos. Organizations like Moderna show us the path forward: integrated leadership that views human potential and AI as complementary forces rather than competing priorities. The question isn't whether this evolution will happen, but whether your organization will lead it or be left assembling yesterday's pieces while tomorrow's opportunities slip away.

CHAPTER 12

YOUR IGNITION ASSIGNMENT

"We are called to be architects of the future, not its victims"

– Buckminster Fuller

Right now, someone in your orbit has potential that could change everything. They might be the team member everyone writes off as "difficult." The intern whose ideas get dismissed. The colleague who's given up proposing solutions because nobody listens.

You've spent this entire book learning to unlock your own potential, developing self-leadership, building competence that creates passion, riding the AI dragon, and finding confident humility. But mastering these capabilities was never the end goal. It was preparation for this moment: becoming the spark that ignites excellence in others.

This is your graduation from student to teacher, from passenger to driver, from sparked to igniter.

Welcome to your final assignment.

THE DAY DISNEY'S RISING STAR LEARNED TO LISTEN

Wanda Rau thought she understood leadership. Fresh from leading Disney's consumer products division in India, Wanda had just been promoted to oversee markets across Southeast Asia, the Middle East, and Australia. She was confident, articulate, and ready to scale her success. Then her new leader called with some feedback: "Wanda, you speak too fast. The team cannot understand what you're saying."

For someone who prided herself on good communication, this felt devastating. "I believe that I'm very articulate and can get my message across," she recalls thinking. But instead of defending herself or dismissing the feedback, Wanda made a choice that would transform her from a successful manager to a true igniter of human potential.

This is the first test every potential igniter faces: Will you let feedback about your own limitations become fuel for understanding others' struggles?

Months later, when Wanda met with her team face to face, they laughed about the communication issue. "I wish you had just told me this," she said. "The most important thing for a leader is to be able to communicate, right? And to be able to use the words that resonate with your audience. Not the words that resonate with me."

That moment became the foundation for everything that followed. "The big takeaway from that was that I have always managed to steer myself in the right direction of the market that I'm leading and the audience that I'm leading. So since then, it's always been about them and less about me."

The igniter's first principle: Transformation begins when you stop trying to be understood and start working to understand.

This shift from self-focused to other-focused leadership soon faced its ultimate test. Wanda inherited a team member who was, by all accounts, incredibly talented but challenging to work with. Internal and external stakeholders would indirectly tell her, "How it was not easy to work with this team member."

Here's where most leaders choose the easy path: manage the person out, reassign them, or simply tolerate the dysfunction. But igniters see something different in difficult people. They see untapped potential waiting for the right conditions to flourish.

Wanda chose the harder path, the igniter's path. "I spent a lot of time talking to them," she explains. "I had the privilege of traveling around Asia, sometimes once a week, most definitely twice a month. I would have conversations that would run into hours."

The igniter's second principle: Potential development requires investment of your most precious resource, time.

But Wanda wasn't just putting in time; she was investing strategically. She sought to understand not just what this person was doing wrong, but why they were doing it. "I got a deep understanding of where they came from and why they did or said what they did, and with that empathy, I got them to make a change."

The igniter's third principle: Sustainable change requires addressing beliefs, not just behaviors.

The breakthrough came when that team member said, "Okay, Wanda, I get you. I know you trust me and believe I can be the change. Can you help me?" This wasn't just behavioral compliance, it was identity transformation. The "difficult" team member had become someone who saw themselves as capable of positive change.

From Sparked to Igniter – The IGNITE Blueprint

Wanda's journey from feedback receiver to potential igniter reveals more than just personal growth; it provides a precise roadmap for how anyone can become an igniter using the IGNITE framework you've mastered throughout this book.

Wanda unconsciously applied each element of IGNITE to transform from someone who managed people to someone who ignited their potential. Here's how you can do the same.

INSPIRE: Shift from Self-Focus to Other-Focus

Your Igniter Action: Stop asking "How can I look good?" and start asking "How can I help others discover what's possible?" True inspiration emerges when people feel you genuinely care about their success more than your own recognition.

Implementation: In your next team interaction, listen for the moment when someone's voice changes, when they talk about something they care about. That's their spark. Reflect it back to them: "When you talked about X, I could see you light up. Tell me more about that."

GUIDE: INVEST TIME IN UNDERSTANDING, NOT JUST DIRECTING

Your Igniter Action: Replace quick fixes with deep understanding. Most managers give advice; igniters ask questions that help people discover their own insights.

Implementation: Schedule regular one-on-ones focused entirely on understanding, not managing. Ask: "What's really challenging you right now?" "What would success look like to you?" "What support would help you thrive?"

NURTURE: BUILD BELIEF AND BELONGING THROUGH EMPATHY

Your Igniter Action: Create psychological safety, where people feel safe to be imperfect while growing. Show that you believe in their potential even when they don't believe in themselves.

Implementation: When someone struggles, resist the urge to fix immediately. Instead, say: "I believe you have the capability to figure this out. What would need to be true for you to succeed here?"

INTEGRATE: COMBINE UNDERSTANDING WITH ACTION

Your Igniter Action: Help people see how their existing strengths can be recombined in new ways. Don't just identify weaknesses to fix; identify strengths to amplify.

Implementation: Ask your team member: "What are you naturally good at that you might not even realize?" Then: "How could we apply that strength to this new challenge?"

TRANSFORM: TURN RESISTANCE INTO PARTNERSHIP

Your Igniter Action: Stop trying to change people and start creating conditions where they choose to transform themselves. The goal isn't compliance; it's partnership in their own development.

Implementation: When you encounter resistance, pause and ask: "What would need to change for this to feel like an opportunity instead of a burden?" Listen to their answers and co-create solutions.

EVALUATE: MEASURE TRANSFORMATION, NOT JUST PERFORMANCE

Your Igniter Action: Measure identity change, not just behavior change. Ask: "How has this person's view of themselves shifted?" rather than just "Did they complete the task?"

Implementation: In follow-ups, ask: "How has this experience changed how you see yourself?" and "What new possibilities do you see for yourself now?"

THE IGNITER'S COMPLETE TRANSFORMATION

This is why Wanda's story matters for your journey. She demonstrates that becoming an igniter isn't about having perfect leadership skills from the start. It's about systematically applying the IGNITE framework to shift from managing tasks to developing people.

Notice the progression:

1. **Personal feedback** (her speaking too fast) led to **self-awareness**
2. **Self-awareness** led to **other-focus** (INSPIRE)

3. **Other-focus** led to **investment of time** (GUIDE)
4. **Time investment** led to **empathy and trust** (NURTURE)
5. **Trust** enabled **co-creation** (INTEGRATE)
6. **Co-creation** sparked **voluntary transformation** (TRANSFORM)
7. **Transformation** created **lasting impact** (EVALUATE)

Your Reflection Questions:

- Which element of IGNITE feels most natural to you as a potential igniter?
- Which element challenges you most?
- Who in your sphere is waiting for someone to apply this framework to help them discover their potential?

The Multiplier Effect: After 27 years in corporate leadership, Wanda left Disney to launch her own venture focused on "Empowering human creativity and problem-solving for a digital world." This transition from corporate leader to entrepreneur represents the final stage of becoming an igniter: moving from igniting potential within existing systems to creating entirely new systems for igniting potential in others.

Your Ignition Assignment: Take one person in your sphere and consciously apply the IGNITE framework over the next 30 days. Use Wanda's example as your guide, but make it your own. The person whose potential you ignite will become living proof that you've mastered not just personal potentialization, but the higher calling of igniting excellence in others.

The INSPIRE Element – Why Authenticity Ignites Potential

Wanda's transformation shows us the complete IGNITE framework for becoming an igniter. But mastering the first element, INSPIRE, often requires overcoming our deepest fear: that we need to be perfect to lead others.

Most aspiring igniters get stuck right here. They think: "How can I inspire someone else when I'm still figuring things out myself?" or "I need to have it all together before I can help others grow."

This thinking is not just wrong, it's just backwards. The most powerful igniters don't inspire through perfection. They inspire through what I call "courageously human leadership." And no one demonstrates this better than Marina Traub.

Marina's journey reveals a counterintuitive truth about the INSPIRE element: your willingness to be authentically imperfect gives others permission to discover their own authentic potential.

We met Marina when we first introduced the Potential Proprioception model; she was the competitive rower who nearly burned out from pretending everything was fine when it wasn't.

But Marina's real breakthrough wasn't just personal. It was discovering that her own struggle to be authentic could become the spark that ignited transformation in others.

When the world shut down in 2020, Marina made a decision that seemed simple but proved revolutionary. She started teaching yoga online for free. Not because she was trying to build a business or establish herself as a guru, but because she was doing what felt true: creating space where people could drop their performance and connect with themselves.

"People need leadership because it helps to have someone go first," Marina explained. "Like half of what I do is get people comfortable thinking about their pelvis. You know, it's just a set of bones, guys. This doesn't have to be a thing."

Notice what happened: Marina's willingness to be real about uncomfortable topics gave others permission to be authentic. When she admitted her struggles with the "little, tiny whiny part" of herself that's "still scared and doesn't trust the world," people felt safe acknowledging their fears.

Marina discovered something profound about igniting potential in others: **you don't inspire people by being perfect. You inspire them by being courageously human.**

This revelation transforms how we think about the INSPIRE element.

- **Traditional Leadership:** "I must have all the answers before I can lead."
- **INSPIRE Element:** "My honest journey gives others permission to begin theirs."

Marina's approach to igniting potential is deceptively simple: "Your job is just to create a space where people can come closer to themselves, whatever that means for them at the time."

She feels successful when someone laughs in her yoga class or ignores her instructions to do their own version. "Ultimately, I want them to find their own way, not follow mine."

This is a masterful application of the INSPIRE element: creating conditions where people discover their own potential rather than trying to mold them into your vision.

Marina's understanding of authentic inspiration led her to create the Radical Re-Entry Project, helping elite athletes transition from external validation to self-leadership. These people have had sports coaches tell them whether they've had a good day for 10, 15, or 20 years.

"When you transition out of that, you have no idea if what you've done is enough," Marina explained.

The breakthrough happens when someone finally stops waiting for permission to trust themselves. Marina's story illustrates a fundamental truth about leadership in the age of AI: people don't need more information or optimization. They need someone to show them it's safe to be authentically human. They need leaders who go first to drop the mask, acknowledge their struggles, and choose alignment over achievement.

Why This Matters in the AI Age

Marina's story illustrates a fundamental truth about leadership in the age of AI: **people don't need more information or optimization. They need someone to show them it's safe to be authentically human.**

As AI handles more of our thinking, the most valuable leadership skill becomes modeling what it means to be fully human: messy, uncertain, vulnerable, and real.

Marina proves that this isn't a weakness, it's the kind of strength that ignites potential in others.

Marina's INSPIRE principle: *"The courage to be imperfectly human in front of others gives them permission to discover their own authentic potential."*

Marina shows us that the INSPIRE element isn't about having charismatic speeches or perfect success stories. It's about the rare courage to go first – to be human in a world that often demands we pretend to be machines.

When you master this element of IGNITE, you don't just inspire others to perform better. You inspire them to be more authentically themselves. And that's where real potential begins to emerge.

In addition to inspiration, to be an IGNITER, you also need to master the NURTURE element, creating psychological safety where people feel safe to grow, especially during times of uncertainty and change.

And there's no greater test of the NURTURE element than helping people navigate their deepest fears about the future. That's exactly what Steve Cadigan discovered when organizations started implementing AI.

The Mirror We're Afraid to Look Into

When organizations rush to implement AI, they often focus on the wrong problem entirely. Steve Cadigan, who has

guided companies through countless technological trans-
formations, sees this pattern everywhere. What he's learned
reveals why the NURTURE element becomes critical during any major change.

Steve Cadigan echoes what James Taylor said in the
last chapter: "What I think we're getting wrong about AI
is that this is more of a cultural challenge than a technical
challenge."

The real issue isn't whether AI can do the work; it's
whether humans can handle what that means for their identity, values, and future. Steve's insight reveals a fundamental
truth about the NURTURE element: **when people feel
psychologically threatened, their potential shuts down.**

The Psychology of Fear VERSUS Growth

Steve uses the parallel of the outsourcing movement, when
jobs were being shifted overseas because they were cheaper,
but employees at the home base saw no benefit to them, and
so they engaged in passive resistance.

"Now we're seeing the same dynamic with AI but amplified." He told me. "People aren't just worried about their
jobs moving to another country; they're worried about their
jobs disappearing entirely, replaced by algorithms that never
sleep, never complain, and never ask for raises."

This is where most leaders fail at the NURTURE element. They treat fear as irrational rather than addressing
the legitimate concerns underneath it.

Steve's NURTURE approach: *"acknowledge before
you advance."*

Steve advocates for a fundamentally different approach that demonstrates masterful NURTURE: "We have to just be open with ourselves that this moment of AI is a threat to a lot of people on a real visceral level."

Instead of dismissing fears, he acknowledges them. Instead of pushing harder, he creates space for honest conversation. This is the NURTURE element in action during technological transformation.

His reframing strategy: "Let's have those conversations and start trying to frame them from how can we make your life more amazing, your career more beautiful, your successes more dynamic with AI. Not how do we squeeze you for more widgets, not how do we grind you to the bone with AI."

The NURTURE Principle for Igniters

Steve's example shows us that the NURTURE element requires:

1. **Acknowledging legitimate fears** rather than dismissing them.
2. **Creating space for honest conversation** about change.
3. **Reframing challenges as opportunities** for human flourishing.
4. **Starting with psychology, not technology.**

Your NURTURE Element Application: Before you can ignite someone's potential, you must first create conditions where they feel safe to be vulnerable about their fears and limitations. This is especially crucial when helping people navigate change or uncertainty.

Steve shows us how the NURTURE element creates psychological safety during change. But safety alone doesn't unlock potential. Once people feel secure enough to engage, you need to master the GUIDE element, asking the right questions that lead people to their own discoveries rather than giving them your answers.

Scott McArthur's painting exercise demonstrates this principle with stunning simplicity.

The Guide Element – The Power of The Right Question

Scott McArthur stands before his Oxford students, pointing to a classical painting on the wall. The reaction is predictably modern: glazed eyes, subtle phone checks, the universal body language of polite disinterest.

"I'm not interested," one student declares, speaking for the room.

Here's where most teachers would make the GUIDE element mistake: launching into a lecture about why they *should* be interested, providing information they didn't ask for, trying to convince rather than discover.

Scott doesn't argue. He doesn't launch into a lecture about artistic appreciation or cultural literacy. Instead, he asks a simple question that changes everything: **"Okay. But if you were interested, what would you see?"**

The Transformative Power of Hypothetical Questions

The question hangs in the air. The students look puzzled and then slightly annoyed. They're being asked to engage with something they've already dismissed. But Scott waits. He has nothing else to do, and, eventually, neither do they.

Slowly, reluctantly, they begin to look, really look, at the painting.

"Why is he looking that way?" one student ventures.

"Why is she holding that object?" another asks.

"What's happening in the background?"

Within minutes, the same students who proclaimed disinterest lean forward, asking questions and building theories about the story unfolding in the artwork.

Why the GUIDE Element Works

Scott's question works because it demonstrates three core principles of the GUIDE element:

1. **It removes the pressure of immediate judgment.** By acknowledging their disinterest upfront, Scott eliminates the need for students to pretend enthusiasm they don't feel. This psychological safety allows genuine curiosity to emerge.

2. **It reframes the challenge.** Instead of "You should be interested in this," the question becomes "What would interest look like?" This shifts from external pressure to internal exploration.

3. **It trusts the process over the outcome.** Scott doesn't need them to love art by the end of the exercise. He needs them to discover their own capacity for deeper observation and questioning.

THE GUIDE ELEMENT FOR IGNITERS

Scott's approach reveals the essence of the GUIDE element: most people aren't lacking curiosity or capability; they're lacking the right conditions for engagement. The guide's job isn't to change people, it's to transform their relationship to the challenge.

"The beauty of some types of art," Scott explains, "is that there's a story in that piece, but you've got to work for it. You can't just look at it and see it. You've got to find it."

This applies perfectly to igniting potential in others. The potential is already there. Your job as a guide is to ask questions that help them discover it themselves.

YOUR GUIDE ELEMENT TOOLKIT

Instead of saying: "You should be excited about this opportunity." **Try asking:** "If you were excited about this, what would you see in it?"

Instead of saying: "Here's what you need to improve." **Try asking:** "What would mastery look like in this area?"

Instead of saying: "You have so much potential." **Try asking:** "When do you feel most alive and capable?"

THE AI-AGE CONNECTION

In the age of AI, when technical skills become increasingly automated, this capacity to ignite human curiosity and engagement becomes one of our most valuable leadership capabilities. The future belongs not just to those who can spot obvious talent, but to those who can awaken the talent that doesn't yet know it exists.

Scott's GUIDE principle: *"The right question at the right moment can transform someone's entire relationship with their own potential."*

We have explored how to INSPIRE through authenticity (Marina), create safety through NURTURE (Steve), and unlock discovery through GUIDE (Scott). But potential only becomes performance when someone actually makes the leap from knowing to doing, from possibility to reality.

This is where the TRANSFORM element becomes crucial – and it's the element most igniters struggle with because it requires something that feels counterintuitive: you must transform yourself first if you want to give others permission to transform.

Sophia Aguilar's journey reveals a profound truth about the TRANSFORM element: **your willingness to courageously change your own life becomes a beacon that gives others permission to change theirs.**

THE TRANSFORM ELEMENT – BECOMING THE CHANGE THAT GIVES PERMISSION

Most people think courage is something you either have or don't have, a character trait some are born with while others live in fear. Sophia Aguilar understood something different: courage is contagious, and it spreads through witnessing rather than words.

Before transitioning at 57, she built a successful marketing company in Mexico, representing major airlines and destinations in the United States. Outwardly, she was thriving. Internally, she carried the weight of not living authentically. But what makes her story essential for understanding the TRANSFORM element isn't just her personal courage, it's how her transformation created ripple effects that gave others permission to change.

Sophia's decision wasn't sudden. It was the culmination of decades spent studying others who had walked similar paths. "I watched from afar," Sophia explains. "It was still part of my lonely process."

During the pandemic, she spent countless hours watching documentaries about people who had faced significant fear to live authentically.

The first TRANSFORM principle: Before you can model change for others, you must study change in others.

Sophia wasn't just gathering information, she was absorbing proof that transformation was possible. Each story she studied became evidence that authentic living was achievable despite fear and social pressure.

"I love this phrase: feel the fear, but do it anyway," she reflects. "Everybody has done things they feared. If people made a list of what they did when afraid, like asking someone on a date or riding a roller coaster, they would deserve medals."

What Sophia discovered applies far beyond gender transition. She found role models demonstrating that authentic living was possible despite fear and social pressure. This principle works for anyone considering significant life changes: career pivots, starting businesses, or any major transition. The key is finding people who faced similar fears and moved through them.

When Sophia finally transitioned, something remarkable happened that demonstrates the TRANSFORM element's power: Rather than facing rejection, she found acceptance and curiosity. "I was very pleasantly surprised because people were very encouraging. They wanted to be part of my transition."

Her business relationships deepened rather than diminished. "Now I have become a celebrity of sorts within the travel industry. Everybody wants to meet with me."

The second TRANSFORM principle: Your authentic transformation often receives more support than your fearful imagination predicts.

But the most significant discovery was yet to come.

The most powerful aspect of Sophia's transformation wasn't personal, it was social. She discovered that her courage had created a new responsibility: Sophia had become what she once needed: a role model for others facing similar fears.

People began calling her for advice. Her willingness to transform had given others permission to consider their own changes. This reveals the core of the TRANSFORM element.

The third TRANSFORM principle: Your personal transformation becomes a proof of concept that others can reference when facing their own need to change.

UNIVERSAL APPLICATION

Sophia's example applies far beyond gender transition. The TRANSFORM element works for any significant change:

- The executive who leaves corporate security to start a non-profit inspires others to align work with values.
- The parent who returns to school at 45 shows others that learning never stops.
- The entrepreneur who admits failure and tries again demonstrates that setbacks aren't endings.
- The leader who shows vulnerability gives permission for others to be human at work.

The pattern is always the same: someone courageously makes a change that seemed impossible, and their transformation becomes evidence that change is possible for others.

For igniters, the TRANSFORM element requires two levels of courage:

1. **Personal Transformation.** You must be willing to change yourself first. You can't ignite transformation in others from a place of stagnation.

2. **Modeling Transformation.** You must be visible about your change process, sharing both struggles and successes so others can learn from your journey.

Sophia's courage to transform herself created ripple effects that gave others permission to change. But transformation without measurement remains invisible. How do you know if your efforts to ignite potential are actually working? How do you scale your impact beyond one-on-one interactions? How do you move from randomly sparking individuals to systematically developing an entire ecosystem of potential?

This is where the EVALUATE element becomes crucial – and it's often the most overlooked aspect of becoming an igniter. Most people focus on the dramatic moments of transformation but miss the systematic approach needed to create lasting, scalable impact.

Jessica Fontana's journey from Meta executive to founder of the Women Leaders Circle demonstrates exactly how the EVALUATE element works: measuring impact, scaling success, and creating systems that ignite potential at an exponential level.

THE EVALUATE ELEMENT – MEASURING AND MULTIPLYING YOUR IMPACT

Jessica Fontana understood something that most aspiring igniters miss: **individual transformation is beautiful, but systematic transformation changes the world.**

When she left her leadership role at Meta, she didn't just want to help a few women develop their potential, she wanted to architect an entire ecosystem where women could ignite excellence in each other.

The first EVALUATE principle: measure identity shift, not just skill development.

"Our vision is to elevate women leaders. They are the pillars of our society, and we believe that increasing the level of equity in terms of leadership and entrepreneurship will impact families, organizations, and society." Notice what she's measuring: not just individual career advancement, but systemic change across multiple levels; families, organizations, society. This is EVALUATE thinking at its most sophisticated.

The second EVALUATE principle: track the multiplier effect.

Jessica doesn't just measure how many women she personally develops. She tracks how many women each participant goes on to develop. "We are creating an ecosystem to elevate their personal and professional development journey and to find a network where they can elevate their potential."

The key word here is "ecosystem," a self-sustaining system where igniters create more igniters.

Jessica's strategic EVALUATE approach:

1. **Individual Level: Confidence and Communication.** "It all starts with their confidence and then their ability to communicate. When public speaking, they must communicate that they're worthy self-leaders and leaders."

Jessica identified the two foundational metrics that pre-dict someone's ability to ignite others: internal confidence and external communication ability. Without these, even talented people can't effectively ignite potential in others.

2. **Network Level: Connection and Collaboration.** "We are creating an ecosystem. . . to find a network where they can elevate their potential." She doesn't just develop individuals – she develops relationships between indi-viduals that create ongoing support and accountability.

3. **Systems Level: Scalable Impact.** The Women Lead-ers Circle operates through "mentoring, academies, and impactful events." Each method serves different aspects of development while creating multiple touchpoints for measurement and adjustment.

THE EVALUATE ELEMENT IN ACTION: GLOBAL SCALE

Geographic Impact Measurement. Jessica tracks not just local impact but global reach: "We are already inspiring excellence in women from Portugal, Italy, Mozambique, South Africa, France, and the United States."

This reveals sophisticated EVALUATE thinking: true impact crosses cultural and geographic boundaries. If your ignition methods only work in one context, they're not robust enough.

Inclusive Impact Measurement. "It's made for the purpose of equity, but men, organizations, companies, and everybody else are part of the solution. And we are up for equity, not just for women."

Jessica measures whether her system creates positive-sum outcomes, where developing one group doesn't diminish others but elevates the entire ecosystem.

With such a mission, I was happy to donate my time to be a mentor in this ecosystem. The Women Leaders Circle is part of Nova University (Portugal), which demonstrates another crucial EVALUATE element: institutional validation and systematic support. This provides several EVALUATE advantages:

- **Credibility metrics** through academic association
- **Systematic feedback** through academic evaluation
- **Scalability infrastructure** through institutional support
- **Long-term sustainability** beyond individual founder energy

Jessica's approach embodies the following quote:

"If your actions inspire others to dream more, learn more, do more and become more, you are a leader"
— *John Quincy Adams*

In our rapidly changing world, the EVALUATE element becomes even more crucial. As AI handles more analytical tasks, human leaders must become better at measuring and developing the uniquely human capabilities that create lasting change.

Jessica's focus on confidence, communication, and community building represents exactly the kind of human development that becomes more valuable, not less, as AI advances.

The Complete IGNITE Framework for Igniters

You now have the complete roadmap.

- **INSPIRE** like Marina: authenticity gives others permission to be real.
- **GUIDE** like Scott: the right questions unlock hidden potential.
- **NURTURE** like Steve: safety creates space for growth during change.
- **INTEGRATE** like Wanda: combine insights with action strategically.
- **TRANSFORM** like Sophia: personal change models possibility for others.
- **EVALUATE** like Jessica: measure and multiply your impact systematically.

Each element builds on the others, creating conditions where human potential naturally emerges and spreads. This is how movements start – not with grand declarations, but with systematic application of principles that awaken what's already there and help it grow exponentially.

You're no longer just someone who has been sparked. You're ready to become someone who sparks excellence in others, at scale, with measurable impact that extends far beyond your individual reach.

The Human Edge in an AI World

As AI handles more routine thinking, something interesting happens: we're forced to become more distinctly human. Theoretical physicist Michio Kaku points out that what separates us from other species isn't just intelligence but our obsession with the future. "We daydream. We see the future, we predict the future, and animals do not," he explains.

This future-oriented thinking becomes crucial as we partner with AI. Machines excel at processing what exists now, but humans excel at imagining what could exist tomorrow.

Brooks Cole puts it perfectly: "People are going to need to step up and become more human, wiser, and more compassionate to be equal to the task of managing this level of intellectual power that AI represents."

The promise isn't that AI will replace human consciousness but that it will amplify it. By freeing us from routine cognitive tasks, AI creates space for higher-order thinking, deeper connections, and more meaningful work. The question isn't whether our tools will become more powerful, but whether our wisdom will keep pace.

Record producer Rick Rubin shared a powerful insight: the most significant breakthroughs in history didn't come from reason, they came from belief, from what he calls "delusion."

The Wright brothers couldn't prove flight was possible through data. They had something AI will never possess:

the capacity to believe in the impossible. This isn't foolishness, it's the source of all human breakthroughs.

As AI advances, we don't become less valuable, we become more essentially human. While machines process information, we architect stories. While algorithms optimize, we dream of what doesn't yet exist.

Your journey to potentialize begins with this uniquely human gift: the audacious belief that things can be better than they are. That you can be better. That the person whose potential you're about to ignite can become extraordinary.

That belief, call it delusion if you want, is what changes the world.

As anthropologist Margaret Mead reminds us: "Never doubt that a small group of thoughtful, committed citizens can change the world; indeed, it's the only thing that ever has." With AI as our ally, that potential for positive change multiplies exponentially.

The future belongs to those who can harness technology's power while staying grounded in what makes us uniquely human: our capacity for love, meaning, and moral choice.

YOUR INVITATION

The stories in this chapter aren't just for inspiration; they're invitations. Every person whose potential you've witnessed being ignited started with someone who made a choice. Someone who saw possibilities where others saw problems. Someone who chose patience over convenience, belief over skepticism, investment over indifference. That someone can be you.

Here's what happens next: as you ignite potential in one person, you become more attuned to potential everywhere. You start seeing gifts instead of gaps, possibilities instead of problems. And the person whose potential you ignited? They begin igniting others.

This is how movements start: not with grand declarations, but with one person deciding to see and develop potential in another.

Your moment is now. Your person is waiting.

BIBLIOGRAPHY

Antal, L. (2009). *A best-in-class mentoring program.* https://www.riversoftware.com/cases/sodexo-mentoring/.

Bandura, A. (1977). Self-efficacy: Toward a unifying theory of behavioral change. *Psychological Review*, 84(2), 191–215.

Bandura, A. (1986). *Social Foundations of Thought and Action: A Social Cognitive Theory.* Prentice-Hall.

Blumberg, M., & Pringle, C. (1982). The missing opportunity in organizational research: Some implications for a theory of work performance. *The Academy of Management Review*, 7(4), 560–569.

Bousquette, I. (2025, May 12). Why Moderna merged its tech and HR departments. *The Wall Street Journal.*

Brown, B. (2010). *The Gifts of Imperfection.* Hazelden Information & Educational Services.

Bryant, A. (2021). *The New Leadership Playbook: Being Human Whilst Successfully Delivering Accelerated Results.* Ocean Reeve.

Bryant, A., & Kazan, A. (2012). *Self-Leadership: How to Become a More Successful, Efficient, and Effective Leader from the Inside Out.* McGraw Hill Professional.

Cambell, J. (1986). *The Inner Reaches of Outer Space.* New World Library.

Chouinard, Y. S. (2012). *The Responsible Company.* Patagonia Books.

Cipolla, C. (2021). *The Basic Laws of Human Stupidity.* Doubleday.

Clark, D. (2013). *Reinventing You: Define Your Brand, Imagine Your Future.* Harvard Business Review Press.

Clark, A., & Chalmers, D. (1998). The extended mind. *Analysis*, 58(1), 7–19.

Csikszentmihalyi, M. (1990). *Flow: The Psychology of Optimal Experience*. Harper & Row.

Csikszentmihalyi, M. (2008). *Flow: The Psychology of Optimal Experience*. Harper Perennial Modern Classics.

Davis, J. (2019, October 15). A radical way of unleashing a generation of geniuses. *Wired*.

DiMasi, J., Grabowski, H. G., & Hansen, R. W. (2016). Innovation in the pharmaceutical industry: New estimates of R&D costs. *Journal of Health Economics*, 47, 20–33.

Duhigg, C. (2016, February 28). What Google learned from its quest to build the perfect team. *The New York Times Magazine*.

Eden, D., & Shani, A. B. (1982). Pygmalion goes to boot camp: Expectancy, leadership, and trainee performance. *Journal of Applied Psychology*, 67(2), 194–199.

Eisenberger, N. I., & Lieberman, M. D. (2004). Why rejection hurts: A common neural alarm system for physical and social pain. *Trends in Cognitive Science*, 8(7), 294–300.

Englert, P. (2023). *Futureselves: Free Will, the Self, and the Science of Living Well*. Ethics Press.

Feldheim, D. (2024). *Lead Like a Girl*. Rowman & Littlefield.

Fildes, A., Mallan, K. M., Cooke, L. et al. (2015). The relationship between appetite and food preferences in British and Australian children. *International Journal of Behavioural Nutrition and Physical Activity*, 12, 116.

Gallwey, T. (1974). *The Inner Game of Tennis*. Random House.

Gladwell, M. (2008). *Outliers: The Story of Success*. Little, Brown & Co.

Gotian, R. (2022). *The Success Factor: Developing the Mindset and Skillset for Peak Business Performance*. Kogan Page.

Hamilton, D. D. (2019). *Cracking the Curiosity Code: The Key to Unlocking Human Potential*. Dr. Diane Hamilton LLC.

Harris, S. (2012). *Free Will*. Free Press.

Hinton, G. (2024). *Banquet speech*. Nobel Prize Outreach 2025. NobelPrize.org.

Jonsson, N. (2020). *Executive Loneliness*. Evolve Systems Group.

Jung, C. (1977). *Symbols of Transformation*. Princeton University Press.

Kahnerman, D. (2013). *Thinking. Fast and Slow*. Farrar, Straus and Giroux.

Kaku, M. (2014). *The Future of the Mind: The Scientific Quest to Understand, Enhance, and Empower the Mind*. Doubleday.

Keagan, R. (1982). *The Evolving Self: Problem and Process in Human Development*. Harvard University Press.

Klein, K., & Peter, C. (2007). *Workplace loyalties change, but the value of mentoring doesn't*. https://knowledge.wharton.upenn.edu/podcast/knowledge-at-wharton-podcast/workplace-loyalties-change-but-the-value-of-mentoring-doesnt/.

Lopata, A. (2020). *Just Ask: Why Seeking Support is Your Greatest Strength*. Panoma Press.

McKinsey & Company. (2010). *Risk Management in Financial Services: Lessons from the Crisis*. McKinsey Global Institute.

Mitra, S. (2005). Acquisition of computing literacy on shared public computers: Children and the "hole in the wall". *Australasian Journal of Education Technology*, 21(3). https://doi.org/10.14742/ajet.1328.

Nadella, S. (2017). *Hit Refresh: The Quest to Rediscover Microsoft's Soul*. Harper Business.

Page, S. (2007). *The Difference: How the Power of Diversity Creates Better Groups, Firms, Schools, and Societies*. Princeton University Press.

Pentland, A. (2012, April). The new science of building great teams. *Harvard Business Review*.

Platow, M. J., Haslam, S. A., & Reicher, S. D. (2015). The social psychology of leadership. In S. G. Harkins, K. D. Williams, & J. Burger (eds.), *The Oxford Handbook of Social Influence* (pp. 339–358). Oxford University Press.

Rosenthal, R. & Jacobson, L. (1968). *Pygmalion in the Classroom*. Holt, Reinhart, & Winston.

Salesforce. (2019). *Ethical & humane use of technology*. https://www.salesforce.com/company/ethical-and-humane-use/

Schrage, M. K. (2025, January 16). Philosophy eats AI. *MIT Sloan Management Review*.

Schutte, N. S. (2019). Increasing curiosity through autonomy of choice. *Motivation and Emotion*, 43, 563–570.

Seligman, M. (2006). *Learned Optimism: How to Change Your Mind and Your Life*. Vintage.

Shelby Clark, A. G. (2019). Fostering adolescent curiosity through a question brainstorming intervention. *Journal of Adolescence*, 75, 98–112.

Sinek, S. (2009). *Start with Why: How Great Leaders Inspire Everyone to Take Action*. Portfolio.

Stephens, G. S. (2010). Speaker–listener neural coupling underlies successful communication. *Proceedings of the National Academy of Sciences*. http://doi.org/10.1073/pnas.1008662107

Tedeschi, R. G., & Calhoun, L. (2013, September 24). Tempered by fire. *Psychology Today*.

Tett, G. (2021). *Anthro-Vision*. Random House.

Tomsky, A. (2024). *Inner Drive: From Underdog to Global Company*. Independently Published.

Youssef-Morgan, C. M. (2024). Psychological capital and mental health: Twenty-five years of progress. *Organizational Dynamics*, 53, 101081.

AI NOTICE

Claude.ai has been used to edit this book for structure and clarity. I have checked all quotes from Claude for accuracy and rewritten them with my own voice.

INDEX